J

Revenge

Annihilating the Spirit
of Athaliah

By Jennifer LeClaire

Copyright

Jezebel's Revenge - Annihilating the Spirit of Athaliah
Copyright © Jennifer LeClaire 2021

Unless otherwise noted, Scripture quotations are taken from the New King James Version.

Table of Contents

1

Athaliah's Diabolical Family Tree

JEZEBEL. SHE WAS A NEFARIOUS QUEEN who murdered the Old Testament prophets, but the spirit that drove her is alive and well. Indeed, Jezebel's entire biological tree is diabolical, starting at least as far back as her demon-worshipping father, continuing with her God-provoking husband and into her generations.

Indeed, the children of Jezebel and Ahab carried an unsavory combination of their wicked traits. If Jezebel was evil in her own right and Ahab was evil in his own right—and they were—then it should come as no surprise that their children walked in depravity multiplied. And the spirit that was on Jezebel's daughter, Athaliah, was perhaps the most depraved of all. Athaliah is one of the cruelest, if not the cruelest, monarchs in Israel's history.

You are probably familiar with Jezebel, the queen who personified a spirit we see manifesting throughout the pages of the Bible and culminating in the end-times church. You may have read my books *The Spiritual Warrior's Guide to Defeating Jezebel, Jezebel's Puppets or Satan's Deadly Trio*. But you may be less familiar with the Athaliah connection. In order to understand the stealth attacks of Athaliah, we need to explore Jezebel's family tree. Before we can lay the axe to the root of this demonic tribe, we have to understand the fruit of the operations of the spirits that drove these satanic clans.

1

JEZEBEL'S IMMEDIATE INSIDIOUS FAMILY

Before Jezebel ever was her parents were. Strangely, there is nothing in the Bible or the pages of history about Jezebel's mother. Jezebel's mother is an absolute mystery. We know she existed but there's not a trace of evidence about her. Did she die in childbirth? Did her husband abandon her and take the kids? Was she murdered?

Indeed, I've searched high and low, far and wide and cannot find a trace of Jezebel's mother, not in church history books, concordances, theological articles or commentaries. It's as if she's been completely wiped from history—and we don't even know why. I imagine Jezebel had emotional issues that opened her up to demonic suggestions, and really didn't know how to be a mother to her sons and daughters. And we know every girl needs her mother. Athaliah, then, had a terrible role model for a mother.

We do read in the pages of the Bible about Jezebel's father, Ethbaal. He was a king of the Sidonians and a Baal worshipper (see 1 Kings 16:31). Historian Josephus reveals him as a priest Astarte. Astarte, or Ashtoreth, is also known as the Queen of Heaven. This is the God of the Canaanites (see Jeremiah 44). Astarte was a goddess of war and seduction. It's easy to see Jezebel took on these characteristics—and you'll see throughout the pages of this book that Athaliah did too.

Ethbaal had plenty of blood on his hands and was a coup-maker. Ethbaal usurped the throne of Tyre by assassinating Pheles, according to *Smith's Bible Dictionary*. In other words, Jezebel's father gained his crown, position and power by murdering a sitting king. The wicked spirits Ethbaal served inspired murder in his heart. Without a mother,

Ethbaal was Jezebel's main influence in life. Doubtless, she heard the story of her power-hungry father's shortcuts to power.

If that's not telling, this is where it gets interesting. Jezebel's brother, Baal-Eser inherited the throne from his idolatrous father. Baal-Eser's son, Mattan, later took over for him. Mattan's son was Pygmalion and his sister was Dido. Scholars such as F.M. Cross indicate Dido, Athaliah's niece, fled from her brother after he stole her inheritance. Historians say Dido founded the ancient city of Carthage in 813 B.C. Dido later changed her name to Isabella. So a blood relative of Queen Jezebel founded an entire city and served as its ruler after her brother stole her inheritance.

You can see the treachery and the quest for power in this royal family line. Doubtless, Athaliah had the same "anything for power" mindset that ran in her generations. You'll connect all these generational dots in Athaliah's life through the pages of this book. Keep in mind Astarte, Baal, Jezebel, and Athaliah are all symbolic of ancient spirits that still roam the earth. We see the spirits that operated through the two queens—different but similar spirits—moving again strongly in the New Testament in the Book of Revelation.

JEZEBEL'S PROVOKING HUSBAND

You are probably at least somewhat familiar with Ahab. King Ahab seemed hell-bent on provoking God from the moment he ascended to the throne. His first recorded move was to marry Sidonian King Ethbaal's daughter Jezebel and serve her gods (see 1 Kings 16:31). Ahab did more to provoke God to anger than any other king before him (see 1 Kings

16:33). The provocation started when he married Jezebel for political reasons instead of love.

Ahab then allowed Jezebel, in a sweeping religious reform, to bring Baal and Ashtoreth worship to new heights in Israel. He not only broke the second commandment by worshipping Baal he also broke the third commandment by building wooden images, a temple, and an altar for Baal in Samaria (see 1 Kings 16:32)—all to please Jezebel. Ahab and Jezebel were religiously correct on the outside, even naming many of their children Jewish names. They had a form of godliness but did not pledge allegiance to the one true living God, Jehovah.

If that were not enough, Ahab stood by and watched while Jezebel massacred the prophets of the Lord (1 Kings 18:4). It wasn't as if Ahab was an Old Testament New Ager who worshipped this, that, and the other god. Ahab made his choice of gods clear when he did nothing to protect Jehovah's true prophets, or come against Jezebel for massacring them.

Jezebel was a persecutor of the one true living God's followers. She wasn't content with Jehovah as a god among many gods. She wanted to murder anyone who pledged allegiance to God and God alone. And she used her position in Ahab's kingdom to execute her will as he willfully worshipped her gods. She manipulated his authority to carry out her agenda. Ahab empowers Jezebel by giving her the authority to flow freely.

Ahab was sold out to Jezebel and her will. He seemed loyal to Jezebel and Jezebel alone. When Elijah defeated the 850 false prophets at the Mount Carmel showdown, Ahab ran back and told Jezebel immediately. Ahab also footed the bill to keep Jezebel's prophets living in luxury. Jezebel's prophets were on the state payroll and lived the high life—all in exchange for telling Jezebel what she wanted to hear.

Catch this: Jezebel employed 450 prophets of Baal and 400 prophets of Asherah, according to *The Dakes*. Even if feeding them only cost $15 a day, which is a low estimate, keeping these false prophets on the payroll would cost the Kingdom of Israel $12,750 a day. That's $89,250 a week, $357,000 a month, and nearly $4.3 million a year. Ahab financially supports Jezebel's murderous agenda.

AHAB'S JEZEBELIC USURY

Of course, Ahab realized certain benefits by allowing Jezebel to usurp his kingship. Indeed, Jezebel gave him what he wanted to placate his lusts, including setting up innocent Naboth and having him murdered so a depressed Ahab could stake claim to his vineyard (see 1 Kings 21). Ultimately, serving Jezebel and her gods instead of the God of Israel cost Ahab his life and the lives of his sons. Ahab uses Jezebel to do his dirty work.

Ahab was a lover of Jezebel, a lover of himself, a lover of power—he did not receive the love of the truth (see 2 Thessalonians 2:10). Not only is Ahab not a lover of the truth, but he also makes an enemy out of anyone who tells him the truth or who stands for God. After God sent a famine to the land of Samaria, Ahab called Elijah a "troubler of Israel" (1 Kings 18:7). Elijah set the record straight, telling Ahab he was the one who was troubling Israel "in that you have forsaken the commandments of the Lord and followed the Baals" (1 Kings 18:18). After Ahab stole Naboth's vineyard, the Lord sent Elijah to deliver a message to him.

"So Ahab said to Elijah, 'Have you found me, O my enemy?'" (1 Kings 21:20). And let's not forget Micaiah. He wouldn't prophesy what Ahab wanted to hear and it landed him in prison (see 1 Kings 22).

Earlier, we discussed how Ahab broke the second and third commandments. But he also broke the tenth commandment. He coveted what belonged to his neighbor— he coveted Naboth's vineyard and used Jezebel to get it for him. We know that Ahab was rebellious against the Word of God because he consistently broke the law. And, of course, idolatry was the sin that opened the door.

Ahab was an emotional mess. When he didn't get his way, he wore his emotions on his sleeve. Ahab was sullen and angry, for example, when Naboth wouldn't sell him his vineyard (see 1 Kings 21:14). Ahab manifested insecurity, which is why he kept the "yes-men" prophets around him (see 1 Kings 22) and why he allowed the strong-willed Jezebel to usurp his authority. Ultimately, Ahab catered to his emotions rather than to his spirit. He was led by the lusts of the flesh rather than the Spirit of God.

FALSE REPENTANCE RISING

False humility is one thing. False repentance is another. When the Lord sent Elijah with a word of condemnation to Ahab, he appeared to repent but it was false. Elijah prophetically spoke these words, "'Behold, I will bring calamity on you. I will take away your posterity, and will cut off from Ahab every male in Israel, both bond and free. I will make your house like the house of Jeroboam the son of Nebat, and like the house of Baasha the son of Ahijah, because of the provocation with which you have provoked Me to anger, and made Israel sin.

And concerning Jezebel the Lord also spoke, saying, "The dogs shall eat Jezebel by the wall of Jezreel." The dogs shall eat whoever belongs to Ahab and dies in the city, and the birds of the air shall eat whoever dies in the field.

1 Kings 21:23-24

How did Ahab respond?

He humbled tore his clothes and put sackcloth on his bod, and fasted and lay in sackcloth, and went about mourning.

1 Kings 21:27

Although the repentance put off God's judgment, Ahab's heart really didn't change. It's like the kid who says he's sorry because he got caught but goes out and does the same thing again. Ahab rent his garments but not his heart. We know this because Ahab did not forsake his idols, he did not return Naboth's vineyard to its rightful heirs, and he did not bring Jezebel in order. He went on in the next chapter to put Micaiah in prison because he wouldn't prophesy according to the party line. Ultimately, actions speak louder than words. Ahab remained Jezebel's puppet until the day he died.

JEZEBEL'S SINISTER CHILDREN

Ahab and Jezebel had many children. In 2 King see Ahab had 70 sons. The Bible describes three some detail: Athaliah, Ahaziah, and Jehoram, v about originally in *Jezebel's Puppets*. A Scriptu Jezebel's evil influence on their lives.

7

According to *Smith's Bible Dictionary*, the name Athaliah means "afflicted of the Lord" and *Easton's Bible Dictionary* defines the name as "whom God afflicts." Athaliah actually murdered her own grandchildren to gain power (see 2 Chronicles 22:11), outdoing the evil of her wicked mother. We'll dive more deeply into who Athaliah is in the next chapter.

Another of Jezebel's offspring was Ahaziah. His name means "held by Jehovah," according to *Easton's Bible Dictionary*. He took after Ahab but was clearly influenced by his evil mother—Jezebel taught him to worship Baal and Ashtoreth. Ahaziah was the eighth king of Israel, succeeding Ahab after he was killed in battle. But he learned nothing from his parents' demise. He consulted with false gods for counsel when he was sick instead of turning his heart to God, another manifestation of the false prophetic connected to Jezebel (see 2 Kings 1:2).

Finally, Jehoram was Ahaziah's brother. He was king of the northern kingdom of Israel and ruled 12 years (see 2 Kings 3:1). Although *Smith's Bible Dictionary* defines his name as "whom Jehovah has exalted" and *Hitchcock's Bible Names Dictionary* defines Jehoram as "exaltation of the Lord," he did not live up to his name. Indeed, Jezebel taught him to worship Baal and he practiced idolatry. At one point, Elisha tried to help Jehoram by revealing Syria's battle plans but he later turned on the man of God and actually vows to kill him just as Jezebel wanted to kill Elijah (see 2 Kings 6:31). Like mother, like son.

The lesson here is that we need to be cautious not only Jezebel, but also Jezebel's children—or in our day Jezebel's itual children. Christians who sit under a ministry where

Jezebel rules can take on the characteristics of Jezebel even if they aren't flowing in a full-blown Jezebel spirit.

BEWARE THESE TAG-TEAMING SPIRITS

In my book, *Satan's Deadly Trio*, I wrote about how the spirits of religion, Jezebel and witchcraft tag team to attack believers. Of course, that's not the only demonic tag team in the spiritual warfare world. What better combination than mother-daughter spirits? We see the spirit of Jezebel and Athaliah working together in the life of John the Baptist.

Remember how the Old Testament Queen Jezebel was after Elijah's head? Elijah called showdown at Mt. Carmel. Jezebel sent a messenger to Elijah saying, "So let the gods do to me, and more also, if I do not make your life as the life of one of them by tomorrow about this time." Of course, Queen Jezebel never got the prophet Elijah's head. But the spirits of Jezebel and Athaliah tagged team against John the Baptist, whom Jesus called "the Elijah who is to come" (Matthew 11:14). The spirit of Elijah was on John the Baptist. The spirit of Ahab was on Herod. The spirit of Jezebel was on Herodias. And the spirit of Athaliah was on Herodias' daughter. Mark 6:16-29 gives the account:

> *But when Herod heard, he said, "This is John, whom I beheaded; he has been raised from the dead!" For Herod himself had sent and laid hold of John, and bound him in prison for the sake of Herodias, his brother Philip's wife; for he had married her. Because John had said to Herod, "It is not lawful for you to have your brother's wife."*
>
> *Therefore Herodias held it against him and wanted to kill him, but she could not; for Herod feared John, knowing that*

he was a just and holy man, and he protected him. And when he heard him, he did many things, and heard him gladly.

Then an opportune day came when Herod on his birthday gave a feast for his nobles, the high officers, and the chief men of Galilee. And when Herodias" daughter herself came in and danced, and pleased Herod and those who sat with him, the king said to the girl, "Ask me whatever you want, and I will give it to you." He also swore to her, "Whatever you ask me, I will give you, up to half my kingdom."

So she went out and said to her mother, "What shall I ask?"

And she said, "The head of John the Baptist!"

Immediately she came in with haste to the king and asked, saying, "I want you to give me at once the head of John the Baptist on a platter."

And the king was exceedingly sorry; yet, because of the oaths and because of those who sat with him, he did not want to refuse her. Immediately the king sent an executioner and commanded his head to be brought. And he went and beheaded him in prison, brought his head on a platter, and gave it to the girl; and the girl gave it to her mother. When his disciples heard of it, they came and took away his corpse and laid it in a tomb.

You can't come against Jezebel without experiencing revenge from Jezebel's daughter.

ANCIENT SPIRITS STILL OPERATING TODAY

Revelation 2:20 exposes that the same spirit who influenced Jezebel's family will be at work in the end-times church—actually teaching the people of God the depths of Satan. This spirit is Jezebel. Where you find Jezebel, you will often find Ahab and Athaliah. Revelation 2:18-25 offers Jesus' words to the church in Thyatira:

> *I know your works, love, service, faith, and your patience; and as for your works, the last are more than the first. Nevertheless I have a few things against you, because you allow that woman Jezebel, who calls herself a prophetess, to teach and seduce My servants to commit sexual immorality and eat things sacrificed to idols.*
>
> *And I gave her time to repent of her sexual immorality, and she did not repent. Indeed I will cast her into a sickbed, and those who commit adultery with her into great tribulation, unless they repent of their deeds. I will kill her children with death, and all the churches shall know that I am He who searches the minds and hearts. And I will give to each one of you according to your works.*
>
> *Now to you I say, and to the rest in Thyatira, as many as do not have this doctrine, who have not known the depths of Satan, as they say, I will put on you no other burden. But hold fast what you have till I come. And he who overcomes, and keeps My works until the end, to him I will give power over the nations...*

Remember that as you read this book. You can overcome Jezebel. You can overcome Athaliah. You carry authority. Now let's learn how to use it.

2

Who Is Athaliah?

WHO IS ATHALIAH? This spirit is not much talked about—and she likes it that way. Demons are neither male nor female, but I call Athaliah she just because this spirit worked most predominantly through a female in the bible. However, let's be clear: Like Jezebel, Athaliah can work through a male or female.

Athaliah has stayed under the radar screen of mainline spiritual warriors. But make no mistake: while many still have a hard time believing there is a real Jezebel spirit, the spirit of Athaliah is gaining momentum and wreaking real havoc on the lives of those who don't see her. The hour has come when Athaliah is rising and attacking at new levels. Ignorance of this demon will bring much destruction to churches, families, and lives.

I hadn't heard much teaching on Athaliah when I bumped into this demon—and I haven't heard much teaching on it since. Again, Athaliah likes it that way. If she can stay hidden in the shadows—if she can keep us ignorant to her existence—she can operate without much resistance. But our ignorance does not make us immune to the reality of this stealth satanic agent. It's a lie that ignorance is bliss. In fact, ignorance could be deadly. That's why Paul warned us not to be ignorant of the devil's devices.

2 Corinthians 2:11 (AMPC) tells us, "For we are not ignorant of his wiles and intentions." The New Living

Translation puts it this way: "For we are familiar with his evil schemes." The Message says, "We are not oblivious to his sly ways." And The Passion Translation emotes, "For we know his clever schemes." Athaliah, like other demon powers, has wicked wiles, infuriating intentions, evil schemes, sly ways and clever manipulations. The agenda of any demon is to steal, kill and destroy (see John 10:10). Athaliah goes about it a little differently than some other spiritual enemies.

LYING IN WAIT

OVER THE YEARS, I've seen a few articles that mentioned Athaliah but when I began to study this spirit for myself in the pages of the Bible, my eyes were opened to a level of warfare that was familiar yet altogether different than what I had encountered over the previous twenty years. This spirit is lying in wait, and few see it. And some of what is taught is so extrabiblical that it can't be trusted.

Indeed, I have discerned by the spirit and by practical experience that this spirit is rising and attacking and we aren't seeing it. We are either blaming the attack on some other spirit—or some other person—or we don't know enough about spiritual warfare at all to equate our troubles with a spiritual attack. I keep saying "we aren't seeing it" because we aren't seeing it. But in the pages of this book, you will see it clearly. You will discern it accurately. And you will overcome it completely.

The late Lester Sumrall once said Jezebel will be one of the main spiritual enemies of the end-times church. I believe he was right, and I believe that's why Jezebel appears in Revelation 2—the last book about the last of the last days before the victorious Second Coming of Christ. But, again, what we've largely missed is the reality of Jezebel's daughter. The Lord has shown me that the spirit of Athaliah is running alongside Jezebel. Together, this mother-daughter duo delivers a one-two punch with enough synergy to drive a technical knockout in spiritual warfare. You'll find yourself reeling from the attack. You won't know what hit you unless you know what hit you.

Practically speaking, here's one way you bump into this spirit. Let's say you find yourself in a battle with Jezebel. You enter into a spiritual wrestling match. You employ the skills you've learned and execute your spiritual authority and throw Jezebel down. You gain the victory. Then, seemingly out of nowhere Athaliah strikes.

You may think you didn't defeat Jezebel and reemploy the same strategy, trying to push Jezebel back again. But that doesn't work because you're not dealing with Jezebel anymore. You made a presumption in the spirit and you're growing battle weary. You're really dealing with Athaliah, who looks a lot like Jezebel but is not. You can't come against Jezebel without experiencing revenge from Jezebel's daughter.

Battling Athaliah takes a different strategy. Again, it's not the same spirit. Again, Athaliah looks a lot like Jezebel. Athaliah may act a lot like Jezebel. But Athaliah is not Jezebel

WHO IS ATHALIAH?

So who is Athaliah? Athaliah came from the royal line of Omri, the sixth king of Israel. With parents who sought political alliances to advance their kingdom, Athaliah was given in marriage to Jehoram, the eldest son of Judah's King Jehoshaphat (2 Kings 8:18). Jehoshaphat would probably rethink that marriage if he had it to do over again. (Be careful who you marry!)

I wrote a book a few years ago in which I mentioned Jezebel and Athaliah. I asserted Athaliah is even more wicked than Jezebel. A young editor wanted to argue with me on the point, insisting I could not put that in the book because it's just my opinion. Hmm. Well, 2 Chronicles 22:11 said Athaliah murdered her own grandchildren, which went far and above anything Jezebel ever did. Jezebel was a killer, but she never killed her own family. That makes Athaliah more wicked than Jezebel.

According to *Smith's Bible Dictionary*, the name Athaliah means "afflicted of the Lord," and *Easton's Bible Dictionary* defines the name as "whom God afflicts." That seems like a fitting name for a daughter of this wicked queen. But it gives you a hint—God always sees Athaliah as a defeated foe. The Lord sees all of our enemies as defeated foes. That's because Jesus triumphed over them on the cross. Colossians 2:14:15 reads, "Having disarmed principalities and powers, He made a public spectacle of them, triumphing over them in it." However, we have to enforce Christ's victory with His powerful name and delegated authority.

JEZEBEL'S MINI-ME

Athaliah is somewhat like Jezebel's "mini-me," a younger version of another who closely resembles the original. I have a daughter. She looks kind of like me. She talks kind of like me. She even walks with a similar gate. But she's not me. In fact, she's a little shorter and has blond hair. Though she shares some of my characteristics, she has a distinct personality. She's got her own ways. She is not a carbon copy.

You may find you've taken on some of the features, beliefs, mindsets, and behaviors of one or both of your parents. My dad is very analytical and he has a dry sense of humor. I am the same way. My mother is very compassionate and generous. I am the same way. There may be things, though, that we don't like in our parents that we, unfortunately, emulate anyway because it was modeled to us. But I am not my mother. I am not my father. Athaliah is like her mother Jezebel but is not her mother. Athaliah is like her father Ahab, but she is not her father.

Athaliah learned from her mother's wicked ways. I imagine she watched her mother as she plotted against the prophets of Jehovah. She may have been listening in the other room while Jezebel conjured up a plan to falsely accuse Naboth and steal his vineyard to appease a covetous Ahab. She may have watched Jezebel paint her face in preparation of confronting Jehu. She may have seen her dad sulking and refusing to eat or disrespecting the prophet Elijah.

Pulpit Commentary tells us,

We find in this woman, Athaliah, the infernal tendencies of her father and her mother, Ahab and Jezebel. Though they had been swept as monsters from the earth, and were now lying in the grave, their hellish spirit lived and worked in this their daughter. It is, alas! often so. We have an immortality in others, as well as in ourselves. The men of long-forgotten generations still live in the present. Even the moral pulse of Adam throbs in all.

ATHALIAH IN ACTION

What does the spirit of Athaliah look like in action? We'll explore that in-depth in the pages of this book. But to give you a quick summary: Athaliah is a murdering, self-advancing spirit—much like Jezebel but perhaps even more vicious. You need discernment in this battle because, at first glance, Athaliah looks like Jezebel. I can't stress that enough. You need to know your enemy before you can truly defeat your enemy. You don't want to, as Paul said, beat the air. And you don't want to pick a fight with a demon that's not bothering you. Like me, I'm sure you have enough warfare without stirring up devils that don't have you on their radar screen.

The generational bloodline of Ahab and Jezebel was beyond wicked. It was as if their children had the worst parts of both of them, but Athaliah stands out in the Bible because she did the unspeakable—she murdered her own family for power. As you read the pages of this book, don't go on a witch hunt, seeing these traits in people and calling them Athaliah's. While Athaliah can influence people, many times this battle is in the heavens. And even if you do face someone under Athaliah's influence, your battle is not against flesh and blood.

Athaliah is representative of the spirit that influenced the wicked queen of Judah. She carries the characteristics of the demon that influenced her. I do not know what God calls this spirit, but we use Athaliah to describe the workings of this spirit. Think about it this way: Long before doctors agreed to name cancer, the disease was raging and killing people. Somebody had to decide to name it so the medical community would have a common vernacular with which to fight it. We call this spirit Athaliah.

3

When Athaliah
Attacked Me

ALTHOUGH I HAD PROBABLY FACED WHAT I CALL "Athaliah warfare" for decades without knowing what it was because I was unaware this spirit existed, Athaliah tipped her hand after I got back from Nigeria. My first known-battle with Athaliah started when I accepted an assignment in Africa.

I was invited to go to Nigeria to help with a School of the Prophets. When I flew into Lagos, the most populous city in the nation and all of Africa, I didn't sense any unusual warfare—which was unusual since we had several people at Awakening House of Prayer, the South Florida church I pastor, warn us about the intense witchcraft.

Don't get me wrong. I understood all too well I was stepping into a city steeped with witchcraft. Since I had never been to Africa, I was ready. I was on guard. I was on high alert. I had my armor on and my sword at my side. But as we landed, I felt the peace of God. When we arrived at the airport, we were escorted through customs—skirting the long lines of frustrated people waiting to get home. The ride from the airport to the hotel was smooth. There were no signs of attacks.

That's just the way Athaliah wanted it. This demon is too smart to say hello, at least not face to face. She was waiting in the wings for the opportune time to strike. We were only on the ground in Nigeria for 24 hours. The entire journey was without warfare, save the brief moment when I started teaching the prophets how to battle the spirit of Jezebel. We were praying corporately against the operations of this spirit when suddenly all the lights in the building went out.

In America, many intercessors would have grabbed their purses and ran out the back door if the building went suddenly dark in the midst of such spiritual warfare. Not so in Nigeria. Hundreds of people started praying fervently in tongues and the sound of war invaded the darkness. Within a few minutes, the lights were back on and we were celebrating the power of God that toppled the work of the prince of the power of the air in our midst.

I Exposed Athaliah

In one of my lessons, I exposed Athaliah. I taught the students part of what I am teaching you in this book, but I've learned much more since then about how to defeat this demon. The students were interested but it was such new material I wasn't sure if they really got it. But one thing I would soon come to found out—Athaliah heard it.

After three lessons on Jezebel and one on Athaliah, I was whisked back to the airport to head back home for a spiritual warfare intensive on marine demons. Again, the pathway was smooth. There was no visible warfare. We discussed on the 36-hour flight back how strong the prayer covering must have been to walk in and out without any demonic interference to speak of. It seemed almost too good to be true.

I mean, I understand my authority but with all the warning words, we expected more resistance. At some level,

I wondered if I had made an impact in Nigeria. In my experience, when you are making an impact for God, the enemy resists you or you get retaliation. But nothing. Despite the 36-hour flight home and arriving to my condo late at night, I woke up the next morning feeling well rested and ready to run. I went to Awakening House of Prayer to teach the Drowning Water Spirits intensive. (You can still take the course at schoolofthespirit.tv.)

I was energized. The teaching was strong. Suddenly, in the middle of the teaching, I felt what I can best describe as a python spirit wrapping around my chest. You can actually see it in the intensive teaching because I stopped to battle against it. In that moment, I considered it backlash from exposing these marine demons—and that was part of it. I successfully battled the attack and continued with the teaching.

JEZEBEL'S REVENGE

Wrapping up with my students, I went home and was still alert and energized. I was hungry for the Word of God so I sat in my bright orange prayer chair reading. When it was afternoon coffee time and I got up from the chair to head to the kitchen. I took three steps ... one, two, three ... when I felt something wrap around my ankle like a lasso and pull tightly. I heard a popping sound and my entire foot went numb instantly. I didn't know what hit me.

I hopped backward on one foot to sit down, momentarily stunned. I thought I could shake it off, but my ankle felt frozen. I was unable to move it without excruciating pain. My ankle and foot started swelling up. I've had sprained ankles before, but never like this. I sat for a few minutes assessing. With my foot numb, I wasn't sure if the blood was cut off or what was going on. I called my friend and told her I might need to go to a hospital. (That's not like me but when you can't feel your foot... I've watched enough medical shows to know that if you can't feel a heartbeat in a limb it's not getting any circulation and started thinking the worse as the battle started raging against my mind.)

My friends came over and wrapped it up. It was so excruciating I was almost in tears every time I had to get up to move around. The next morning, I had bruises not just on my ankle, but higher up on my calf. It literally looked like a thick lasso wrapped around my leg twice and squeezed—just as the sensation I had in the spirit when the injury occurred. The swelling refused to go down for weeks. Doctors said it might never go all the way back down.

THE ATHALIAH-PYTHON TAG TEAM

I wrote about how spirits tag team in chapter 1. This is a perfect example. Athaliah-Jezebel-Python worked together. Even still, I didn't immediately recognize Athaliah in the mix. I only saw Python. I was focused on the manifestation of the lasso around my foot and the visible evidence of a spiritual attack in the form of the lasso-like bruises—and thinking about the attack during the marine demons intensive.

In order to truly understand the tag-team dynamics, you have to understand the hierarchy, or ranking, of demons. Paul outlined this hierarchy in Ephesians 12:6-13:

> *For we do not wrestle against flesh and blood, but against principalities, against powers, against the rulers of the darkness of this age, against spiritual hosts of wickedness in the heavenly places. Therefore take up the whole armor of*

God, that you may be able to withstand in the evil day, and having done all, to stand.

After the attack, I could barely stand physically. But kept standing spiritually, keeping every assignment to preach, pray and prophesy in the nations and at home at Awakening House of Prayer in Ft. Lauderdale. I soon discovered that my host in Nigeria also suffered an attack on his ankle, a bad sprain. This was too much of a coincidence. I started praying for more discernment. It took me a few weeks to put the spiritual dots together and see the picture of Athaliah. I still didn't know how to overcome this spirit, but I endured and the attack waned.

A MORE OPPORTUNE TIME

We know from Scripture the enemy always comes back at an opportune time (see Luke 4:13). He waits for the best moment to strike, usually when we're least expecting it. That more opportune time was about seven months later when I was in Singapore. After a devastating personal betrayal in which I was so emotionally compromised my spiritual guard was down, I had to get on a plane and fly across the world to teach on Jezebel for an international satellite TV station. The teaching to expose Jezebel would be translated into 15 languages and be broadcast to almost all of the world.

After the taping on Athaliah, that night I could barely move. My legs were cramping to the point that I was in excruciating pain and my back was aching deeply. This was not normal. I stand up and teach long hours regularly without any issues. My intercessor who traveled with me sat in a chair all day and sustained the same attack. She was not teaching, but she was covering me in prayer and the enemy retaliated.

What happened? Because of the personal betrayal, I was not on high alert against Athaliah. And I paid a price.

Don't get me wrong. I was ready for Jezebel. But I had not yet learned the lesson I am teaching you now. I wasn't ready for the Athaliah attack. For days, I struggled and suffered in deep physical agony. The attack didn't break until we were in the air on a plane between Singapore and Indonesia. Suddenly, all the pain left and I was completely fine—like nothing happened. It was remarkable. We ministered in Indonesia at a megachurch before taking a few days to rest in Bali. When I got home, I received an email from someone who worked on the programs. He said, "I don't know much about it but a spirit came in my room last night and said 'I am Athaliah' and now I can barely walk."

JEZEBEL'S REVENGE

That e-mail made me feel better as I was feeling I had missed it badly. But that wasn't the half of it. The e-mail also spoke of a man in Australia who called and told them that Athaliah has a tendency to attack legs in the natural realm. This was an aha moment. Again, don't get me wrong. I wasn't happy that my friend was attacked. But I was happy for the revelation and confirmation.

You know this: When you are the target of intense warfare, sometimes you feel like you are losing your mind, like you are weak in the spirit, or that you won't gain victory. Athaliah is very bold—so bold that she went to one of the TV staff and overplayed her hand. Remember I said that. The enemy always overplays his hand. We'll talk more about that in a later chapter.

What I learned from that experience is you can't go after Jezebel without experiencing retaliation from Jezebel's daughter. Think about this with your natural mind for a minute. If someone messes with my mother, I take exception to that. Of course, as Christians, we pray for those who use us and bless those who curse us but you get the idea. We have a tendency to take it personally when people mistreat our family. You want to defend them and war for them. Remember, Athaliah is Jezebel's daughter.

From that point on, I pressed in to understand who Athaliah is, what she wants, and how she operates. I studied how she is different than the queen mother Jezebel, where her weak spots are, and the biblical strategy for defeating— or annihilating—Athaliah. That's what I am teaching you in the pages of this book.

4

Athaliah Invaded
My Dreams

I WAS IN A HOUSE THAT WAS UNFAMILIAR TO ME. It wasn't a large house but it was crowded with people—overcrowded. It was almost like a college party house where the living room was overcapacity but nobody seemed to mind. Everyone was enjoying themselves but I could not discern the occasion. I wasn't sure what they were celebrating. It was as if the Holy Spirit picked me up and transported me in the spirit to a faraway place into an event already in progress.

I kept on watching. In this congested home full of Christians people were running to and fro doing I don't know what. The entire house was buzzing with activity, almost as if they were preparing for something. I could not see the faces of these hectic herds. It was as if the Lord was purposely hiding the faces of the people, of which I am sure represent a great number of others.

I kept on watching. I did not speak with anyone. I just kept observing and discerning. I was in the room but it was as if no one could see me. I wasn't sure if I was invisible or if they just didn't notice me. Either way, I was glad I was seemingly invisible. I was grieved, though I did not yet know why. After some time, I was aware people noticed my presence but carried on anyhow.

I kept on watching. No one really spoke to me except one man. I could not see his face either. Since the man engaged in conversation, my journalism instincts took over and I started asking him questions about what was going on. My soul was investigating my spiritual agitation. I was not sure if it was an angel or the Lord. I did not get an immediate answer.

I kept on watching. It was so surreal yet altogether real. After some time, I discerned the people were confined in this house, though they were seemingly unaware of their imprisonment. They went in willingly and had not yet figured out how difficult it would be to escape. The people remained busy doing many things, but not one of them ever went out. Their movement was limited to inside this house. They had no idea that they were trapped. They could not leave.

A CULT COMPOUND

I kept on watching. As I observed, this house reminded me of a cult compound. The people inside were there of their own free will and actually did not want to leave. Their needs were met. They had fellowship. As I said earlier, it seemed like they were enjoying themselves. They were deceived. Fully deceived. But what had deceived them? What happened? What pathway led them into this house?

I kept on watching. After a while, it was mealtime. Food was being distributed on a platter, just like at a party. It wasn't any kind of food I readily recognized. It was strange. After having blended into the background for some time, I was recognized again I was offered something to eat from this platter.

I kept on watching. With a better view, I saw it was a strange-looking piece of meat on the platter. It was oversized on a large bone—and it was one just a single serving. I thought, "No one could eat at one time." Some offered me the meat. I politely declined because it was strange. I instinctively felt that if I ate the meat I would be coming into agreement with whatever was going on there.

I kept on watching. As I looked on, I was disturbed in my spirit as other people accepted this strange food. It was almost like it was a matter of survival because the food that was being offered was the only food available. Yet no one thought it strange. They welcomed it. They devoured it as if it were a filet mignon. Yet I would not eat it. I could not eat it.

RED ALERT

I kept on watching. Suddenly, the party seemed to end. Everyone in the house was on high alert. I could not perceive any immediate danger but people were scrambling around as if something bad were about to happen. I separated myself. I walked down a hall and went into a bedroom. There was an oversized window in the bedroom.

I kept on watching. As I looked outside the window, I saw two women in a car pulling into the driveway. I suddenly knew this was what was causing the alarm in the house. I bent down to stay out of view and kept peeking through the window.

I kept on watching. The two women were carrying something into the house. I could not see them and did not want them to see me. I was trying to discern what was happening. I felt alarmed in my spirit and my adrenaline was flowing. Finally, they saw me. They wanted me to open the door to the house and let them in. Everyone else was hiding. I was the only one that seemed positioned or even willing to let them in. I decided it was safe, that they presented no danger to me, and set out to let them in. Then I woke up.

JEZEBEL UNLEASHED

When I woke up, I realized this dream was not about me, but the Lord was showing me something about the Body of Christ and my role in the situation. After years of praying into this, I have resolved at least part of the interpretation.

I was an observer in the dream, which means I was standing as an intercessor. Houses in dreams often represent ministry. This was a communal house, rather than an individual's home. This was a false camp within the prophetic movement that had been deceived by Jezebel. In other words, these were Jezebel's prophets. I did not recognize the house in the dream because I had never been in it.

The Bible speaks of the prophets of Jezebel. As I wrote in my book, *Discerning Prophetic Witchcraft*, prophets of Jezebel are influenced by the spirit of Ashtoreth. Ashtoreth was the pagan God Queen Jezebel served. Ashtoreth was known as a seducing goddess of war. The prophets of Jezebel prophesy smooth flattering words to try to manipulate and control you. If that doesn't work, they transition into warfare mode and prophesy fearful sayings to try to intimidate and control you. Ashtoreth and Baal were married. So these spirits often share one another's characteristics. We must discern what we are dealing with.

Lester Sumrall once said Jezebel was one of the main spirits the end-times church would have to contend with. It's no coincidence that Jezebel shows up in the Book of Revelation. And it's no accident that the epic war room vision I saw revealed that God was going to dispatch angels to fight death, disease and Jezebel. Prophetically speaking, I believe the angels fighting death and disease are doing so on behalf of believers in the face of coming plagues. I believe the angels battling Jezebel are coming near the end.

THAT WOMAN JEZEBEL

Jesus left a letter for the church at Thyatira. He wrote these words that we must understand if we want to resist the influence of Jezebel. We read this important, relevant letter in Revelation 2:18-29:

> *These things says the Son of God, who has eyes like a flame of fire, and His feet like fine brass: "I know your works, love, service, faith, and your patience; and as for your works, the last are more than the first. Nevertheless I have a few things against you, because you allow that woman Jezebel, who calls herself a prophetess, to teach and seduce My servants to commit sexual immorality and eat things sacrificed to idols.*

> *And I gave her time to repent of her sexual immorality, and she did not repent. Indeed I will cast her into a sickbed, and those who commit adultery with her into great tribulation, unless they repent of their deeds. I will kill her children with death, and all the churches shall know that I am He who searches the minds and hearts. And I will give to each one of you according to your works.*

> *Now to you I say, and to the rest in Thyatira, as many as do not have this doctrine, who have not known the depths of Satan, as they say, I will put on you no other burden. But hold fast what you have till I come. And he who overcomes, and keeps My works until the end, to him I will give power over the nations—"He shall rule them with a rod of iron; They shall be dashed to pieces like the potter's vessels"—I*

also have received from My Father; and I will give him the morning star. "He who has an ear, let him hear what the Spirit says to the churches.

The spirit of Jezebel is real and raging. It has infiltrated some camps of the prophetic movement. We must stay pure. Purity is one of the key defenses against the Jezebel spirit. Where there are unhealed hurts and wounds, they can fester and bring bitterness that attracts Jezebel to be your protector. Prophetically speaking, now is the time to get free from every tie that binds because the warfare is only going to increase in the days ahead.

EATING AT JEZEBEL'S TABLE

After much prayer, I believe the man who spoke to me was an angel. He seemed to be an ally in the house. I inquired of the angel in the dream for explanations, just like prophets in the Bible inquired of angels in their epic visions. I cannot remember what he said. I believe part of that revelation was withheld for another time.

I understand the strange food is food that was coming from Jezebel's table. When Elijah called for the showdown at Mt. Carmel, he instructed Ahab,

Now therefore, send and gather all Israel to me on Mount Carmel, the four hundred and fifty prophets of Baal, and the four hundred prophets of Asherah, who eat at Jezebel's table.

1 Kings 18:19

Just as there were prophets who ate at Jezebel's table in the original false prophetic movement, there are prophets who eat at Jezebel's table in today's false prophetic movement. Thank God there is a remnant, but the false prophetic camp is feeding right on the doctrines of Satan, which Jesus mentioned in the Book of Revelation.

The house in the dream was unfamiliar to me because whatever this prophetic camp is, I have not been up close to it. I have seen a lot of false prophetic functions over the last decades but whatever this is, I have yet to see it closely enough to describe it. Then again, I could not see the people's faces. They could be people we all recognize or people who have not yet made it onto the scene. I hope I never do see the fullness of this dream manifest, but we know Jesus prophesied false prophets would rise in the last days and deceive many. There is no praying away this reality.

STRANGE FOOD, STRANGE FIRE

Any time I am offered food in a dream I won't eat it. In this particular dream the meat represented revelation as a reward for compromising with Jezebel. Remember, the false prophets who ate at her table were living it up in a time of famine. They were on Jezebel's payroll. They were Jezebel's yes-men. The true prophets were either dead at Jezebel's hands, escaped to other countries, hiding in a cave eating bread, or roaming about like Elijah.

Keep in mind meals in the Bible often represent provision, covenant, and even an intimacy in sharing. The people in this home had made a covenant with Jezebel and she was providing for them, a house and food. They had established a level of intimacy with Jezebel. The meat, again, is revelation but what about the bone? A bone in a dream can often represent something that has no spiritual life.

This strange food also represented strange fire. We see the concept of strange fire in Leviticus 10:1-2 (KJV):

And Nadab and Abihu, the sons of Aaron, took either of them his censer, and put fire therein, and put incense thereon, and offered strange fire before the Lord, which he commanded them not. And there went out fire from the Lord, and devoured them, and they died before the Lord.

This was a fatal sin.

What is this strange fire? Strange fire is unauthorized fire. Other translations call it the wrong kind of fire, profane fire, and unholy fire. Aaron's sons did not get their fire from the holy altar of God. Strange fire is more than prophesying out of the soul and innocently thinking it's God. Strange fire "implies not only that they did it of their own proper motion, without any command or authority from God, but that they did it against his command," according to *Benson Commentary*.

A WARNING OF JUDGMENT

In my dream, there was some sort of alarm in the house. The people started to scatter. I believe it was a warning of coming judgment. God judged the strange fire and he will judge Jezebel. Jesus said he will throw her on a sickbed, along with those who commit adultery with her (see Revelation 2:22). These prophets were eating from Jezebel's table and operating in strange fire. Judgment must come, but the time is not yet.

I went into the bedroom, a place of intimacy in a house full of chaos. No one else was there. Intimacy with Jesus will help us avoid the snares of Jezebel. In the dream, I looked through a window, which in dream language often speaks of prophetic perspective. I had seen what is in the living room of the house. From my secret place, looking through a window, I was seeing what is to come.

What puzzled me was the two women pulling into the driveway. I prayed and pondered this and suddenly the Lord took me to Zechariah 5. What unfolded as next took my breath away. I believe the two women represented spirit beings like in Zechariah 5. They were intent on getting in the house and they carried something.

ZECHARIAH'S STARTLING VISION

The following is the account from Zechariah 5:5-11 (NLT):

Then the angel who was talking with me came forward and said, "Look up and see what's coming." "What is it?" I asked. He replied, "It is a basket for measuring grain, and it's filled with the sins of everyone throughout the land."

Then the heavy lead cover was lifted off the basket, and there was a woman sitting inside it. The angel said, "The woman's name is Wickedness," and he pushed her back into the basket and closed the heavy lid again. Then I looked up and saw two women flying toward us, gliding on the wind. They had wings like a stork, and they picked up the basket and flew into the sky.

"Where are they taking the basket?" I asked the angel. He replied, "To the land of Babylonia, where they will build a temple for the basket. And when the temple is ready, they will set the basket there on its pedestal."

As Zechariah meditated on what he saw, an angel of interpretation came forth to help him understand the meaning. Essentially, the angel helped the prophet see how iniquity must be removed from the Holy Land. Consider part of the prophet's ministry is to teach people to separate the profane from the holy (see Ezekiel 44:33).

WHO IS THE WOMAN IN THE BASKET?

Who is this woman in the basket? The angel said her name is Wickedness. When I first had the dream, I thought it was Jezebel. I pondered on this dream for the better part of two years because I did not have enough interpretation to release it to the Body of Christ. This is the first time I have spoken or shared it publicly because I only now see the bigger picture.

Up until now, we've been seeing the prophets of Baal and the prophets of Jezebel. But what is coming as we edge toward the end is even more sinister. In 2018, I underwent one of the most severe, longest-lasting attacks I have ever endured. It was one of the most physically excruciating and the most mentally draining. It was my first major battle with the spirit of Athaliah, Jezebel's daughter.

When I first had this dream, I thought perhaps it was Jezebel in the basket. But, no, it's a spirit more wicked than even the notorious Jezebel. It's the spirit of Athaliah in the basket. Meredith G. Kline confirms this in Kerux, a publication devoted to biblical theology. She also shares this confirmation in her book, *Glory in Our Midst*.

"Surely this embodiment of wickedness in the apostate Athaliah is the historical model behind Zechariah's image of wickedness personified as the woman in the ephah," she writes. Jezebel is quite literally the mother of harlots John writes about in Revelation 17:1-6. Athaliah is one of the most wicked harlots in the Bible. Indeed, Athaliah is more wicked than Jezebel, carrying the traits of her father Ahab—who did more to provoke the Lord to anger than any king before him (see 1 Kings 16:33) and Jezebel.

JEZEBEL'S REVENGE

The wicked Queen Jezebel died at the hand of her eunuchs after Jehu rode furiously toward her dwelling and commanded them to "throw her down!" (2 Kings 9:33) But the spirit that was influencing Jezebel sought revenge. That spirit found revenge through Jezebel and Ahab's daughter, Athaliah. She became the first-ever queen of Israel by murdering all other royal heirs to the throne. Only one, Jehoash, escaped.

According to *Smith's Bible Dictionary*, the name Athaliah means "afflicted of the Lord," and it defines the name as "whom God afflicts." Athaliah actually murdered her own grandchildren to gain power (2 Chronicles 22:11), outdoing the evil of her wicked mother. *Pulpit Commentary* writes:

> We find in this woman, Athaliah, the infernal tendencies of her father and her mother, Ahab and Jezebel. Though they had been swept as monsters from the earth, and were now lying in the grave, their hellish spirit lived and worked in this their daughter. It is, alas! often so. We have an immortality in others, as well as in ourselves. The men of long-forgotten generations still live in the present. Even the moral pulse of Adam throbs in all.

ATHALIAH'S UNLEASHING

Athaliah was the woman in the basket. And the angel pushed her back into the basket and closed the heavy lid again. The angel did this because it was not yet time for this spirit of Athaliah's ultimate uprising. While this spirit has been working in the earth, it is one of Satan's end-times secret weapons to wreak havoc on the church.

Few talk about Athaliah, and the few that do seem to scratch the surface of the depravity of this spirit or how to defeat it. I believe the dream revealed the time of Athaliah's uprising is here. And most believers are unprepared to resist it. For that matter, most believers are not yet ready to accept the reality of the Jezebel spirit, much less this woman named Wickedness.

After the angel pushed Athaliah back into the basket, Zechariah's vision continued. He saw two women flying toward him, gliding on the wind. These were not angels because there are no female angels. Rather, these are a different form of spirit beings. These winged women came from heaven with wings filled with the wind. In Zechariah's vision, they did not take the basket and fly into the sky to Babylon to be set up on a pedestal. In my dream, they took the basket into the house. A temple is a house.

Could I have been in the temple built for Athaliah in my dream? Could it be possible that Athaliah is about to usurp Jezebel in the earth, exacting revenge on the prophets—and operating through some that are as ambitious and bloodthirsty as the Israelite queen we see pictured in the Bible? Could it be possible that the Jezebelic prophets will begin following this greater evil? I believe some already are.

5

A Vengeful Heir

ATHALIAH IS NOT A RIGHTFUL HEIR—she is a vengeful heir. She would stop at nothing to taste the power that eluded her mother, ultimately seeking to take revenge on her mother's behalf. The Jezebel loyalist had no love for her siblings or her children or her grandchildren. She had a love of self and tyranny. Here's the backstory: Jehu set out to take vengeance on the house of Ahab after he was anointed king of Israel. His prophesied mandate is found in 2 Kings 9:7-10:

> *You shall strike down the house of Ahab your master, that I may avenge the blood of My servants the prophets, and the blood of all the servants of the Lord, at the hand of Jezebel. For the whole house of Ahab shall perish; and I will cut off from Ahab all the males in Israel, both bond and free. So I will make the house of Ahab like the house of Jeroboam the son of Nebat, and like the house of Baasha the son of Ahijah. The dogs shall eat Jezebel on the plot of ground at Jezreel, and there shall be none to bury her.*

Jehu started his conquest with two of Ahab's offspring—Joram and Ahaziah—before confronting Jezebel and commanding the eunuchs to throw her down (see 2 Kings 9). After Jezebel's violent death, Jehu went after Ahab's seventy sons in Samaria, then Ahaziah's forty-two brothers, then the rest of Ahab's family and finally the worshippers of Baal. Somehow, Jehu missed Athaliah. We don't know if she hid or if he was more concentrated on the males in the family. But Athaliah escaped Jehu's wrath and subsequently walked in her own wrath in Judah.

JEZEBEL'S POST-MORTEM REVENGE

Jezebel was thrown down and trampled, perhaps as Athaliah looked on from under her bed. Whether she witnessed Jehu's campaign against her mother or not, the death of Jezebel and Ahab caused an unrighteous indignation in Athaliah. Athaliah clearly was not a Yahweh follower. She was not raised in a God-fearing home. If she had any love for Jehovah, the death of her parents along with much of the rest of the family would have spurred repentance.

Put another way, if Athaliah were not sold out to Baal and Ashtoreth worship under her mother's regime, she would have accepted that divine judgment fell on the house of Ahab and sought to mend her ways. Instead, Athaliah chose to retaliate against Yahweh by seeking revenge for the Queen Mother Jezebel . Vengeance is never God's way—and when we seek revenge we are acting like Athaliah. We need to understand how dangerous the revenge mindset is if we want to overcome this demon power in our lives.

Romans 12:19 warns,

Do not avenge yourselves, but rather give place to wrath; for it is written, "Vengeance is Mine, I will repay," says the Lord.

Paul was quoting Yahweh, of which Moses penned in Deuteronomy 32:35:

Vengeance is Mine, and recompense;
Their foot shall slip in due time;
For the day of their calamity is at hand
And the things to come hasten upon them.

Athaliah took justice into her own hands—and she was an unjust judge. She didn't see that the sword of the Lord would one day fall upon her.

DAVID MOVED IN THE OPPOSITE SPIRIT

By contrast, David understood that vengeance belongs to the Lord. David was faced with injustice over and again but never took matters into his own hands. One of the most striking events in David's life is found in 1 Samuel 25 when David was on the run from Saul and sent some of his men to ask Nabal for some supplies.

When Nabal refused in a very offensive way, David was fuming mad and gathered four hundred men with swords to overtake Nabal. David wanted his head. Nabal's wife Abigal heard of the incident and went out to meet David, bringing an abundance of supplies for him and his army and begging forgiveness. David woke up and remembered vengeance is the Lord's. David said to Abigal in 1 Samuel 25:32-34:

> *Blessed is the Lord God of Israel, who sent you this day to meet me! And blessed is your advice and blessed are you, because you have kept me this day from coming to bloodshed and from avenging myself with my own hand. For indeed, as the Lord God of Israel lives, who has kept me back from hurting you, unless you had hurried and come to meet me, surely by morning light no males would have been left to Nabal!*

David went on his way. Abigal went on her way. She found Nabal having a great time, feasting and drinking wine.

> *"So it was, in the morning, when the wine had gone from Nabal, and his wife had told him these things, that his heart*

died within him, and he became like a stone. Then it happened, after about ten days, that the Lord struck Nabal, and he died.

1 Samuel 25:37-38

When David heard of it, he replied, "Blessed be the Lord, who has pleaded the cause of my reproach from the hand of Nabal, and has kept His servant from evil! For the Lord has returned the wickedness of Nabal on his own head" (1 Samuel 25:39). This was a strategic time for David to see the hand of God moving on his behalf, especially so immediately. I believe it informed the next chapter of his life in his dealings with Saul.

DAVID REFUSED TO USURP AUTHORITY

King Saul, influenced by a demon power, tried to kill David over and over again for no other reason than jealousy. David had an opportunity to kill Saul while he was sleeping. It was the second time he had the opportunity to raise himself up as king and fulfill Samuel's prophecy over his life. He wouldn't do it. He knew better.

David's men encouraged him to seize the opportunity to ascend to the throne they felt was rightfully his:

Then Abishai said to David, "God has delivered your enemy into your hand this day. Now therefore, please, let me strike him at once with the spear, right to the earth; and I will not have to strike him a second time!"

1 Samuel 26:8

Instead, David chose to move in the opposite spirit and wait for God to vindicate him and raise him up as king in His perfect timing in His perfect way. 1 Samuel 26:9 reads:

But David said to Abishai, "Do not destroy him; for who can stretch out his hand against the Lord's anointed, and be guiltless?" David said furthermore, "As the Lord lives, the Lord shall strike him, or his day shall come to die, or he shall go out to battle and perish. The Lord forbid that I should stretch out my hand against the Lord's anointed."

ATHALIAH'S BLOODY UPRISING

Athaliah, on the other hand, had no issue stretching out her hand against the Lord's anointed.

Athaliah's son was Ahaziah. He became king of Judah when he was 22 years old but reigned only one year (see 2 Kings 8:25-26). The Bible says, "He walked in the way of the house of Ahab and did evil in the sight of the Lord, as the house of Ahab did, for he was the son-in-law of the house of Ahab" (2 Kings 8:27).

When her son Ahaziah died she seized the opportunity to be the first-ever female queen of Judah. 2 Kings 11:1, reads "Now when Athaliah the mother of Ahaziah saw that her son was dead, she rose up …" Athaliah rose up to a place that Queen Jezebel herself could not attain by establishing herself as queen in Ahaziah's place. Catch that: she established herself.

The Hebrew word for *rose* in this context is not suggesting she stood up and volunteered for a difficult job in a difficult transition. The Hebrew word *arose* speaks of arising in a hostile sense or to "come on the scene." It speaks of confirming oneself, to persist and prove oneself as valid. Athaliah was not the rightful heir to the throne. She was the vengeful heir. This was an insurrection, a coup, an overthrow of the government.

This is what Satan tried to do in heaven. Isaiah 14:12-15 reads, "How you are fallen from heaven, O Lucifer, son of the morning! How you are cut down to the ground, you who weakened the nations! For you have said in your heart: 'I will ascend into heaven, I will exalt my throne above the stars of God; I will also sit on the mount of the congregation on the farthest sides of the north; I will ascend above the heights of the clouds, I will be like the Most High.' Yet you shall be brought down to Sheol, to the lowest depths of the Pit."

Despite Lucifer's failure, haughty demon powers have staged insurrections of families, churches, and companies ever since. Jezebel usurped the king's authority through seduction and manipulation but Athaliah overthrew the true king completely. The rise of Athaliah could be seen as a manifestation of Jezebel's revenge. The rise of Athaliah could be seen as a counter to the double portion anointing that Elisha received from Elisha. Athaliah was even more wicked and rose higher than Jezebel. It almost seems as if she had a double portion of the spirit of Jezebel carried. We always say we want our kids to go further than we did… Jezebel would be proud.

GET VENGEANCE OUT OF YOUR HEART

Before you wrestle with Athaliah, you need to get vengeance out of your heart. That means you need to forgive and let go before you can gain victory in warfare.

If the weapons of our warfare are not carnal—if they are mighty in God for pulling down strongholds as Paul described in 1 Corinthians 10:4—then forgiveness may be among your stealthiest weapon. The enemy never sees it coming. Think about it for a minute. God used forgiveness to deliver us from the enemy's camp. All we have to do is repent and receive that forgiveness to remain free from oppression and condemnation the enemy heaps on our souls when we sin.

But there's another side to that truth: When we walk in forgiveness toward others whose soul and flesh are influenced by demonic powers, the enemy cannot put us into bondage to resentment, bitterness and unforgiveness. When you look at forgiveness through this lens, it becomes a powerful weapon that keeps your heart free and clean. Indeed, obeying God's command to forgive opens the door for God to "punish all disobedience" that caused you harm.

Forgiveness is a double-edged sword. If you do not forgive others, God will not forgive you (Matthew 6:15). Unforgiveness hinders your fellowship with God and affects your anointing. You may still command devils in the name of Jesus, but authentic spiritual authority is diluted when you fail to obey God's command to love people. Love and unforgiveness do not flow from the same spring.

If you do not forgive, it will hinder your prayer life. Jesus said, "Whenever you stand praying, if you have anything against anyone, forgive him, that your Father in heaven may also forgive you your trespasses" (Mark 11:25). Spiritual warfare falls under the umbrella of prayer. How can you effectively bind devils when you yourself are bound with unforgiveness? Unforgiveness puts you at a clear disadvantage on the spiritual battlefield.

OVERCOME EVIL WITH GOOD

Spiritual warfare is more than binding devils in Jesus' name. Spiritual warfare is forgiving those who oppose you, hurt you, or persecute you. And not only forgiving but blessing. And not only blessing but trusting God to avenge you.

In the Sermon on the Mount, Jesus offered revelation on how to deal with people who mistreat you: "I say to you, love your enemies, bless those who curse you, do good to those who hate you, and pray for those who spitefully use you and persecute you, that you may be sons of your Father in heaven" (Matthew 5:44). How can you apply that revelation if you aren't willing to forgive?

Paul wrote,

Beloved, do not avenge yourselves, but rather give place to wrath; for it is written, "Vengeance is Mine, I will repay," says the Lord. Therefore "If your enemy is hungry, feed him; If he is thirsty, give him a drink; For in so doing you will heap coals of fire on his head." Do not be overcome by evil, but overcome evil with good.

Romans 12:19-21

You may not feel like forgiving. You may feel like giving that someone a piece of your mind. You may not feel like blessing your enemy. You may feel like telling the whole town what they did. You may not feel like showing kindness. You may feel like putting your wrath on display. But when you do you give the enemy a toehold, which can lead to a foothold, which can lead to a stronghold.

The weapon of forgiveness is mighty not only to pull down strongholds, but to prevent the enemy from establishing a stronghold in the first place. Indeed, forgiveness is a powerful weapon—one that is too often neglected in our binding and loosing exercises. So before you head to the battlefield, consider that the Lord is long-suffering and slow to anger, and abundant in mercy and loving-kindness, forgiving iniquity and transgression (Numbers 14:18 AMP).

The Lord is a warrior—and He never loses a battle. When you follow His lead and forgive—when you set your heart to overcome evil with good and allow God to take vengeance—you can't lose. Amen.

6

A Maddening Megalomaniac

ATHALIAH WAS A MANIACAL MEGALOMANIAC. She was delusional, convinced her sinister coup de ta would succeed for more than a mere moment in Judah's history. For a brief season, seated on that throne with all its grandeur, she must have felt omnipotent. Surely, she was self-absorbed and narcissistic like her parents—the king and queen of Israel—while she was growing up in Jezreel.

What was modeled to her—the murder and mayhem—undoubtedly emboldened her to make unthinkable moves in her petulant power grab. Again, 2 Kings 11:1, reads, "Now when Athaliah the mother of Ahaziah saw that her son was dead, she rose up...." Another Hebrew word for *rose* is "to be established." Athaliah did not wait for Israel to crown her queen, she took the throne and established herself.

Athaliah called herself the queen just like the Revelation 2:20 Jezebel calls herself a prophetess. No one anointed Athaliah queen, just like no one ordained the end times Jezebel as a prophetess. Athaliah took the throne the way Ahab took Naboth's vineyard—by assumptive force. It seems Athaliah took everything she learned from Ahab and Jezebel and put it into practice. All the manipulation, all the murder, all the misery.

A History-Making Devil

Athaliah became the first-ever woman and only-woman ever to rule Judah. This was the only time the seed of David didn't occupy the throne. Athaliah was beyond a power-hungry woman looking to make history. Athaliah was actually a puppet in a satanic plot to interrupt Messianic prophecy.

Against all odds, Athaliah reigned over the land (see 1 Kings 11:3). Athaliah was the queen of Judah from 841 to 835 BC—that's six terrifying years. We don't know what kind of havoc Athaliah wreaked on Judah during her reign, but we know she did not exalt Jehovah. While Athaliah's reign was a relatively short period in Judah's history, she doubtless did plenty of damage while she sat on the throne by leading Judah into idolatry.

Just as Jezebel usurped Ahab's authority by having Naboth killed, Athaliah usurped her son's authority by seizing the throne and killing any other heirs she could hunt down. It wasn't enough that she was a queen—Athaliah was already a queen in that she had been married to King Jehoram of Judah—she wanted to be the queen supreme, the queen most high, the queen almighty. She wanted a higher title than the one she had. She wanted to be the absolute ruler. She wanted all the glory. God would not stand for it.

Athaliah was vainglorious, narcissistic, pompous, egotistical, high-and-mighty, presumptuous, and everything you'd expect to see in a ruler influenced by demon powers. She exalted herself with no fear of the Lord, failing to understand he would soon humble her. She operated in a level of pride that surpassed her wicked parents and would soon see destruction. It was only a matter of time before

Athaliah was struck down, as pride comes before destruction (see Proverbs 16:18).

SIGNS OF MEGALOMANIA-DRIVEN LEADERSHIP

Athaliah was a megalomaniacal leader. Psychologists would describe this personality as having Machiavellian tendencies, the Napoleon complex, or narcissism. Megalomania is a delusional mental illness that is marked by feelings of personal omnipotence and grandeur, according to *Merriam-Webster's dictionary.* But Athaliah wasn't mentally ill— she was demonized.

Consider this, Jezebel was a narcissist, which is an extremely self-centered person who has an exaggerated sense of self-importance. Megalomania is a step beyond narcissism. For example, Jezebel had a big ego. Athaliah acted like she was actually God. There's a difference between thinking of yourself more highly than you ought and thinking you are untouchable.

Let's take a closer look at this because understanding the behavior of people influenced by an Athaliah spirit will help you discern the root of the attack. Consider these six signs of megalomania as Athaliah manifests them in the pages of the Bible.

1. Feelings of omnipotence: God is omnipotent. He is all-powerful. That's why he's called Almighty (see Revelation 19:6). By taking the queenship into her own hands, Athaliah sought to set herself up as a god. She thought she was unassailable, far above reproach, and absolutely justified. Where Jezebel was power-hungry, Athaliah is power demanding and convinced she is superior to all others. Adolf Hitler may have operated in

conjunction with Athaliah, believing he was the head of a superior race. The deception is that he didn't even carry the characteristics of that so-called superior, or Aryan, race.

2. <u>Narcissistic attitude:</u> Although megalomania is at least one notch above narcissism, all the traits of a narcissist also apply. In many ways, Jezebel may be the classic narcissist. If that's true, you could say Athaliah is Jezebel on steroids. Signs of narcissism include a lack of empathy, the envy of others, arrogance, manipulation, a sense of entitlement, a craving for the admiration of others, and a preoccupation with unlimited success with no possibility of failure.

3. <u>Refusal to admit mistakes:</u> Because the megalomaniac believes he is omnipotent, how could they possibly acknowledge mistakes? Serving under Athaliah's queenship must have been a true terror. If Rehoboam ruled with an iron fist, Athaliah ruled with an iron boot.

4. <u>Fear-mongering:</u> Narcissists want to be loved. Megalomaniacs want to be feared. Although Jezebel works through intimidation of outsiders, Athaliah drives fear among even those closest to her. Imagine the level of intimidation among the inhabitants of Judah when discovered she murdered her own grandchildren to ascend to the throne. If she was capable of such brute force against her own family, what else might she do?

5. <u>Violent tendencies:</u> Where Jezebel had prophets murdered and had Naboth killed, her violence was motivated by personal interests and never compromised her family but rather helped keep her family in power. Again, Athaliah's violent tendencies stripped power

from her family through murder. We don't have a record of other acts of violence Athaliah carried out, but one can imagine the spirit of violence was prevalent in the land because of her headship.

6. Feelings of being indestructible: Because they feel all-powerful and are willing to do anything necessary to exert their will, megalomaniacs also feel indestructible. They don't believe anyone can overcome their plans.

Athaliah, and those influenced at high degrees by this spirit, can be perhaps best described in Psalm 10:4 (NLT), "The wicked are too proud to seek God. They seem to think that God is dead." Or perhaps Athaliah may have said to herself, "God has forgotten, he has hidden his face, he will never see it" (Psalm 10:11, ESV). But Psalm 14:1 tells us the fool says in his heart, "There is no God." Indeed, God is greater than Jezebel and Athaliah—and God sees everything.

7

A Ruthless Murderess

JEZEBEL WAS A RUTHLESS MURDERER. We first read about Jezebel killing off the Lord's prophets while her own yes man prophets sat at her table feasting on food and drink during a time of famine in Israel (see in 1 Kings 18). Jezebel was a murderess from the beginning. As I write in my book, *The Spiritual Warrior's Guide to Defeating Jezebel*:

> If you will not bow down and give the Jezebel spirit what it wants, it will falsely accuse you and murder your reputation as it did Naboth's. If you will not prophesy what saith Jezebel, this spirit will work overtime to cut off your voice—either by putting you in bondage or murdering you—as it did with the prophets of Jehovah. If you confront Jezebel's wickedness, it will threaten to murder you as it did Elijah. Where true authority relies on the law of God to bring justice where justice is due, Jezebel perverts the law of God to bring judgment where judgment is not due.

Jezebel murdered the prophets and ordered Naboth's execution to secure the vineyard wicked Ahab coveted. But, again, Athaliah was even more wicked, murdering her own grandchildren. 2 Kings 11:1 reads: "Now when Athaliah the mother of Ahaziah saw that her son was dead, she rose up and destroyed all the royal descendants."

The Contemporary English Version puts it plainer: "As soon as Athaliah heard that her son King Ahaziah was dead, she decided to kill any relative who could possibly become king." The International Standard Version says, "As soon as Ahaziah's mother Athaliah learned that her son had died, she seized the throne and executed the entire royal bloodline."

In other words, she murdered them. Chances are, she didn't do the dirty deed herself. Rather, she hired executioners and charged them with hunting down and destroying anyone who posed any plausible threat to her insurrection. She ordered the hits. This is why you have to understand the concept of tag team demonic attacks, which I mentioned in the first chapter and will continue to expound upon.

ATHALIAH IS A SPREE KILLER

Athaliah went on a killing spree. The U.S. Bureau of Justice Statistics defines a spree killing as "killings at two or more locations with almost no time break between murders."

Different than a serial killer, a spree killer is methodical. A spree killer is emotional. There is no cooling-off period for the spree killer. Athaliah was a multicide killer. According to Psychology Today, a spree killer faces a precipitating incident that continues to fuel the motivation to kill. In other words, spree killers are on a mission.

Many mass shootings, for example, are rooted in motives like envy or revenge. Tony Farrenkopf, a forensic psychologist who has focused on spree killing profiles, says these criminals often exhibit risk factors like a history of abuse or ineffective parenting. We know Athaliah had some of the worst parents in Bible history. Other traits are a self-centeredness or lack of compassion.

WIPING OUT THE COMPETITION

Let's look at this Scripture again. 2 Kings 11:1 reads: "Now when Athaliah the mother of Ahaziah saw that her son was dead, she rose up and destroyed all the royal descendants." Think about it for a minute: Jezebel wiped out the prophets that were challenging her idolatry.

Athaliah wiped out anyone who could challenge her power. Jezebel had the prophets of God murdered, but Athaliah—both a queen's daughter and a king's wife—murdered her own royal flesh and blood.

Athaliah's motive was power. *Matthew Henry's Commentary* puts it this way: "She thirsted after rule, and thought she could not get to it any other way. That none might reign with her, she slew even the infants and sucklings that might have reigned after her. For fear of a competitor, not any must be reserved for a successor."

Perhaps she wasn't familiar with Leviticus 24:7, "Whoever kills any man shall surely be put to death." Perhaps she didn't realize she was sealing her own fate and she would reap what she had sown. But it's hard to believe she did not hear the command: "You shall not murder" (Exodus 20:13). Athaliah's god wasn't even Astarte or Baal. Ultimately, Athaliah's god was herself.

While Cain killed his brother Abel because of jealousy, Athaliah wiped out her family line because of competition. She wanted to be the last woman standing, the only suitable heir. Athaliah not only had hate in her heart, she let hate move her hands to genocide. She would soon be reminded of Genesis 9:6, "Whoever sheds man's blood, By man his blood shall be shed; For in the image of God He made man."

DON'T ACT LIKE ATHALIAH

If you hope to take authority over Athaliah's attacks, you have to break common ground with the murdering spirit. You might think, I would never murder anyone. But you can murder them with your mind and your mouth. In Matthew 5:21-22, Jesus shared:

> *You have heard that it was said to those of old, "You shall not murder, and whoever murders will be in danger of the judgment." But I say to you that whoever is angry with his brother without a cause shall be in danger of the judgment. And whoever says to his brother, "Raca!" shall be in danger of the council. But whoever says, "You fool!" shall be in danger of hell fire.*

And if you need a confirmation, John spoke these words: "We know that we have passed from death to life, because we love the brethren. He who does not love his brother abides in death. Whoever hates his brother is a murderer, and you know that no murderer has eternal life abiding in him" (1 John 3:14-15).

The battle against Athaliah will be fierce. It may be difficult to separate the principality from the personality—that is, to remember that spirits are influencing people to come against you—but we must remember this truth. Paul reminds us we are not wrestling against flesh and blood—not really (see Ephesians 6:12). And the weapons of our warfare are not fleshly or worldly but they are divine in nature and demolish strongholds (see 2 Corinthians 10:4).

Beyond harboring ill feelings toward someone Athaliah is using them to come against you, we also have to keep a clean heart toward people in general. We act like Athaliah when we release gossip that murders people's reputations or even when we think evil thoughts about them. These evil thoughts are called thought curses.

The preacher said, "Even in your mind do not curse the king; and in your bedchamber do not curse the rich; for a bird in the sky may carry your voice, and a winged creature may declare the matter" (Ecclesiastes 10:20). The word *curse* in that Scripture means, "to make despicable, to curse, to make light, to treat with contempt, bring contempt, or dishonor," according to *The KJV Old Testament Hebrew Lexicon*. The Bible says even in your mind—another translation says in your thoughts—not to curse people. Even in your mind! A word curse gives voice to an evil thought, but how can a thought take voice in the spirit realm?

When we're thinking wrong thoughts about people—or ourselves—we're agreeing with the Accuser of the Brethren. We're getting on the devil's side and allowing him to feed our minds ammunition that will eventually come out of our mouths and become a word curse. Think about it for a minute. If you meditate on how angry and upset you are about someone because they wronged you, how long will it be before you speak out those thought curses and transform them into word curses?

Murder begins in the mind and the heart. Repent before going into battle with Athaliah if you have common ground in this area. Pray this prayer, Father, in the name of Jesus, forgive me for murdering people in my mind and with my mouth. I renounce all agreement with murder and death and

I bless my enemies and pray they will walk in Your perfect will. Help me to fight with your weapons and not in the flesh.

8

An Inheritance Thief

ATHALIAH IS AN INHERITANCE THIEF. This is something else she learned from watching her evil parents, Jezebel and Ahab. In framing Naboth, Jezebel effectively stole his inheritance to deliver to her depressed husband the king. In case you aren't familiar with the story, you'll find it in 1 Kings 21:1-16:

> *And it came to pass after these things that Naboth the Jezreelite had a vineyard which was in Jezreel, next to the palace of Ahab king of Samaria. So Ahab spoke to Naboth, saying, "Give me your vineyard, that I may have it for a vegetable garden, because it is near, next to my house; and for it I will give you a vineyard better than it. Or, if it seems good to you, I will give you its worth in money."*

> *But Naboth said to Ahab, "The Lord forbid that I should give the inheritance of my fathers to you!"*

> *So Ahab went into his house sullen and displeased because of the word which Naboth the Jezreelite had spoken to him; for he had said, "I will not give you the inheritance of my fathers." And he lay down on his bed, and turned away his face, and would eat no food. But Jezebel his wife came to him, and said to him, "Why is your spirit so sullen that you eat no food?"*

> *He said to her, "Because I spoke to Naboth the Jezreelite, and said to him, "Give me your vineyard for money; or else,*

if it pleases you, I will give you another vineyard for it." And he answered, "I will not give you my vineyard."

Then Jezebel his wife said to him, "You now exercise authority over Israel! Arise, eat food, and let your heart be cheerful; I will give you the vineyard of Naboth the Jezreelite."

And she wrote letters in Ahab"s name, sealed them with his seal, and sent the letters to the elders and the nobles who were dwelling in the city with Naboth. She wrote in the letters, saying:

DEMONIC FASTS

"Proclaim a fast, and seat Naboth with high honor among the people; and seat two men, scoundrels, before him to bear witness against him, saying, 'You have blasphemed God and the king.' Then take him out, and stone him, that he may die."

So the men of his city, the elders and nobles who were inhabitants of his city, did as Jezebel had sent to them, as it was written in the letters which she had sent to them. They proclaimed a fast, and seated Naboth with high honor among the people. And two men, scoundrels, came in and sat before him; and the scoundrels witnessed against him, against Naboth, in the presence of the people, saying, "Naboth has blasphemed God and the king!" Then they took him outside the city and stoned him with stones, so that he died. Then they sent to Jezebel, saying, "Naboth has been stoned and is dead."

And it came to pass, when Jezebel heard that Naboth had been stoned and was dead, that Jezebel said to Ahab, "Arise, take possession of the vineyard of Naboth the Jezreelite, which he refused to give you for money; for Naboth is not alive, but dead." So it was, when Ahab heard that Naboth was dead, that Ahab got up and went down to take possession of the vineyard of Naboth the Jezreelite.

This wasn't the only instance in Scripture we find demonic fasts. A group of Jewish people operating under the influence of demon powers sought to murder Paul, engaged in a startling demonic covenant and demonic fast in Acts 23:12-15.

And when it was day, some of the Jews banded together and bound themselves under an oath, saying that they would neither eat nor drink till they had killed Paul. Now there were more than forty who had formed this conspiracy. They came to the chief priests and elders, and said, "We have bound ourselves under a great oath that we will eat nothing until we have killed Paul. Now you, therefore, together with the council, suggest to the commander that he be brought down to you tomorrow, as though you were going to make further inquiries concerning him; but we are ready to kill him before he comes near."

THE STRATEGY OF HOLY FASTS

Let me take a moment here to discuss fasting. God can lead you on a fast before or in the middle of spiritual warfare. Fasting is abstaining from food or some activity to focus on God. South African pastor and author Andrew Murray once said, "Prayer is reaching out after the unseen; fasting is letting go of all that is seen and temporal. Fasting helps express, deepen, confirm the resolution that we are ready to sacrifice anything, even ourselves to attain what we seek for the kingdom of God."

Fasting can help us hear more clearly from God. Fasting helps cleanse your soul of toxic emotions. Fasting helps us crucify our flesh. Fasting can open up wisdom and direction. Fasting can open the door for God's mercy. Fasting can create greater intimacy with God. Fasting can lead you to deliverance. And fasting can also be a prerequisite to successful spiritual warfare.

You remember the story of Jehoshaphat's battle in 2 Chronicles 20. The people of Moab, Ammon and others came to battle against him. The Bible describes it as a great multitude. Jehoshaphat sought the Lord and proclaimed a fast throughout all Judah and prayed. Shortly after, a prophet came with a word about victory in battle through an unconventional strategy.

Battling Athaliah is not conventional warfare. It's extreme warfare. Although I'm outlining strategies in this book, the reality is there is almost always a tag team battle with various other demons means you need prophetic intelligence from the Holy Spirit to ensure your individual victory. Ask the Holy Spirit if fasting is part of the pre-battle strategy to the sensitivity to His Spirit you need to hear the battle plan. Also, check out my book, *101 Tactics for Spiritual Warfare* for biblical tactics the Holy Spirit may lead you to deploy.

ATHALIAH TAKES IT ONE STEP FURTHER

Jezebel stole Naboth's inheritance but Athaliah went into overdrive, stealing the inheritance of all the royal seed. Athaliah's work not only affects a generation but can ripple through generations. Jezebel attacks inheritance but Athaliah kills inheritance and the seed that will bring a future harvest for our children and our children's children.

Proverbs 13:22 reads, "A good man leaves an inheritance to his children's children, But the wealth of the sinner is stored up for the righteous." Instead of generational blessings, Athaliah unleashes generational curses. But like Proverbs 20:21 assures, "An inheritance gained hastily at the beginning will not be blessed at the end."

If Athaliah hadn't had murder in her heart, she could have inherited the land to live on forever (see Psalm 37:29)—perhaps not as the queen but as a queen mother. But her unrighteous behavior would cause the Lord to move against her swiftly. While God gave Ahab and Jezebel about twenty years to repent, Athaliah's Jezebelic revenge would be met with His wrath sooner than she thought. Proverbs 20:21 tells us, "An inheritance gained hastily at the beginning will not be blessed at the end."

BREAKING ATHALIAH'S CURSE

Again, Athaliah's work not only affects a generation but it can ripple through generations. Jezebel attacks inheritance but Athaliah kills inheritance and the seed that will bring a future harvest for our children and our children's children. You may be the one to stop Athaliah's plague on your family line. It's time to break generational curses and activate generational blessings.

Receive this prayer: In Jesus' name,

I break every curse the spirit of Athaliah imposed on my family line through her murderous activities. I take back now the inheritances Athaliah stole in past generations. I reclaim them, now, in Jesus' name and draw a bloodline around my family line. I activate every generational blessing in my family line. Thank you, Lord that I am blessed beyond measure, that I am blessed and cursed not. Let the generational blessings manifest in the name of Jesus.

9

An Illegal
Authoritarian

ALL AUTHORITY COMES FROM HEAVEN. Jesus Himself said,
"All authority has been given to Me in heaven and on earth"
(Matthew 28:18). All true authority, that is. There is an
illegitimate authority and spirits like Athaliah operate in it. I
call it a bastard authority. No one gave Athaliah authority.
She took it.

Athaliah had a domineering, deadly authority that did
not come from heaven—but straight from the hordes of hell.
She operated in a false authority and a false spirit. Ultimately,
she operated in witchcraft. 2 Kings 9:22 speaks of Jezebel and
her witchcrafts. Athaliah operates in witchcraft, which is an
illegitimate authority and power to enforce the will of the god
of this world, the devil.

We know that Satan rules over all rebels, both angels and
demons (see Ephesians 2:1-3). One-third of the angels
followed him in his insurrection that saw the whole group
kicked out of heaven. And humans who do not know the
Lord Jesus Christ as Savior are still under his influence today.
One of the forces he uses is witchcraft.

WHAT IS WITCHCRAFT?

Witchcraft is the power of Satan like the Holy Spirit is
the power of God. Witchcraft is one of the powers listed in

the hierarchy of demons in Ephesians 6:11. I write about this extensively in my book, *Satan's Deadly Trio*. Jezebel's witchcraft is sorcery, which comes from the Hebrew word *magic*. The Hebrew word *magic* means to whisper a spell. In modern church circles, we call these "word curses." We see a clear example of this in Scripture.

Jezebel released a word curse against Elijah when she sent him a messenger threatening, "So let the gods do to me, and more also, if I do not make your life as the life of one of them by tomorrow about this time" (1 Kings 19:2). The result: Elijah was covered in witchcraft, which released imaginations against his mind. The Bible says "when he saw that, he arose and ran for his life, and went to Beersheba, which belongs to Judah, and left his servant there" (1 Kings 19:3). I believe Elijah, being a prophet, saw a fearful vision in his mind and ran after he heard the words of Jezebel's messenger. I believe he saw a picture of the outcome Jezebel was threatening.

This is the same witchcraft in which Athaliah operates. For example, when you think of witchcraft, you probably think of black magic or conjuring the dead. Those abominations are covered in the Bible. But witchcraft is not always so mysterious. Indeed, rebellion, word curses, and works of the flesh also fall into the realm of witchcraft. However you define it, though, practicing witchcraft is a serious sin, and far more Christians are experts at sorcery than you may realize.

Spiritual witchcraft relies on the power of life and death that is in our tongues—and other people's tongues—to release its attacks. The spirits of Jezebel and Athaliah use witchcraft to put you in bondage. I write about overcoming these attacks specifically in *Satan's Deadly Trio*.

YOU HAVE AUTHORITY OVER ATHALIAH

Know this: Athaliah's bastard authority is no match for the authority God gave you in Christ. God has authorized you—He's given you authority. Again, Jesus boldly proclaimed, "All authority has been given to Me in heaven and earth" (Matthew 28:18). Jesus is not a man that He should lie. He wasn't boasting or speaking things that are not as though they were. Jesus is the Co-Creator of the universe. He has preeminence. He has all authority.

One meaning of *exousia*, the Greek word for "authority" in that verse reads: "the power of rule or government (the power of him whose will and commands must be submitted to by others and obeyed." That sums up Christ's authority.

God raised Christ from the dead by the power of the Holy Spirit and seated Him at His right hand in heavenly places, "far above all principality and power and might and dominion, and every name that is named, not only in this age but also in that which is to come. And He put all things under His feet, and gave Him to be head over all things to the church, which is His body, the fullness of Him who fills all in all" (Ephesians 17:22-23).

Now, we are seated with Christ in heavenly places (see Ephesians 2:6). If you are born again, you have been delivered from the power of darkness and translated into Christ's Kingdom (see Colossians 1:13). You've been translated from the enemy's authority and rule of government into Christ's authority and rule of government.

If you don't understand who you are in Christ—if you don't understand your authority in Him—you cannot successfully wage war against the enemy who is waging war against you.

YOU ARE AUTHORIZED

Just like Adam had authority before he handed it over to the devil through his disobedience in the Garden of Eden, we now have authority in Christ to take dominion in the spirit realm over enemies of the cross. Jesus gave His disciples a measure of His own authority, jurisdiction, influence, and anointing so they could go about doing good and heal all who were oppressed by the devil (see Acts 10:38).

Like the disciples, God has authorized you to stand against the enemy. Merriam-Webster offers the world's definition of authority: "power of influence to command a thought, opinion or behavior. But the Greek word for authority in the Bible is *exousia*, which includes the concept of "authorization."

Authority is the power to act on God's Word. When God speaks, we're authorized to move. When you are authorized you are commissioned, certified, licensed, lawful, legitimate, recognized, sanctioned, warranted, and official. Jesus delegated His authority in His name. *HELPS* Word studies reveals "delegated power refers to the authority God gives to His saints authorizing them to act to the extent they are guided by faith (His revealed word)."

We exercise our authority by faith, not by feelings. The authority to demand that the devil loose what belongs to you is yours whether you feel like you've got it or not. You can feel powerless, but the truth is you have the one-two punch of power and authority. Authority has nothing to do with emotions. But you must exercise it for it to be effective.

Jesus has already done everything He's going to do about the devil. He's already done everything He's going to do about sickness. It's up to you to do something now. He is waiting on you to use the authority He gave you to manifest the Kingdom of God in your life.

UNDERSTANDING SUBMISSION TO AUTHORITY

Now here's the catch in spiritual warfare: You need to be under authority to have authority. In other words, you need to submit to God's authority in order to successfully exercise Christ's delegated authority. Jesus Himself said, "I did not come of My own authority, but He sent me (John 8:42). We are not sent forth in our own authority into battle. We must get instructions from God who sends us into battle with His authority.

A Roman centurion—a gentile—demonstrates how understanding the importance of submission to authority is vital in warfare. We read the account in Matthew 8:5-10:

And when Jesus entered Capernaum, a centurion came to Him, entreating Him, and saying, "Lord, my servant is lying at home, sick with paralysis, terribly tormented." Jesus said to him, "I will come and heal him."

The centurion answered and said, "Lord, I am not worthy that You should come under my roof. But speak the word only, and my servant will be healed. For I am a man under authority, having soldiers under me. And I say to this man, "Go," and he goes, and to another, "Come," and he comes, and to my servant, "Do this," and he does it."

When Jesus heard it, He was amazed and said to those who followed, "Truly I say to you, I have not found such great faith, no, not in Israel."

Again, the centurion's understanding of the chain of command and how authority works manifested as faith. Although we don't put our faith in our authority, we put our faith in who we are in Christ, what His Word says about us, and His supreme authority over the devil. Walking in the authority He delegates to us as Kingdom ambassadors of light in the earth is key to victory in spiritual warfare against Athaliah or any other spirit. (Learn more about spiritual warfare in my School of Spiritual Warfare at www.schoolofthespirit.tv.

REVELATION OF AUTHORITY UNLOCKS FAITH TO BATTLE DARKNESS

It's important that you meditate on the authority you have because, like a dog, the enemy can sense when you are walking by fear instead of by faith, doubt instead of belief.

Consider the seven sons of Sceva. Sceva was a Jew and a chief of the priests. As such, his sons were educated in the Word of God. They took it upon themselves to try to cast out evil spirits, saying, "We adjure you by Jesus whom Paul preacheth" (Acts 19:13).

The only problem was, these seven sons of Sceva didn't have faith in the Word of God made flesh. In other words, they didn't have faith in Jesus and had no basis on which to exercise His authority. They didn't have a relationship with Him. They were not born-again. The devils knew they had no authority to use the name. Let's look at the fate of these young men:

And the evil spirit answered and said, "Jesus I know, and Paul I know; but who are ye?" And the man in whom the evil spirit was leaped on them, and overcame them, and prevailed against them, so that they fled out of that house naked and wounded.

Acts 19:15-16

Again, you need a revelation of Christ in you and you in Him to enforce His victory in your life.

Jesus said "occupy until I come" (Luke 19:13). Jesus said to His apostles: "All authority has been given to Me in heaven and on earth. Go therefore and make disciples of all nations, baptizing them in the name of the Father and of the Son and of the Holy Spirit, teaching them to observe all things I have commanded you" (Matthew 28:18-20). Jesus said, "He called His twelve disciples to Him and gave them authority over unclean spirits, to cast them out, and to heal all kinds of sickness and all kinds of disease" (Matthew 10:1).

Before His ascension to heaven, Jesus also said, "In My name they will cast out demons; they will speak with new tongues; they will take up serpents; and if they drink anything deadly, it will by no means hurt them; they will lay hands on the sick, and they will recover" (Mark 16:17-18).

Jesus expects us to enforce His victory in the earth and has equipped us with every weapon we need—and the authority to use His name. But we need a revelation of authority. Just as our Father in heaven revealed to Peter that Jesus was the Son of the Living God—flesh and blood did not reveal that to him—we need a revelation from heaven. Sitting under teachings about our authority helps open our hearts for God's revelation to pour in, but individual study is imperative.

Jesus is the source of our authority: Jesus authorizes us. Our authority lies in the name of Jesus. We can't go toe to toe with the devil in our own right.

God highly exalted Jesus and gave Him the name which is above every name, that at the name of Jesus every knee should bow, of those in heaven and on earth and under the earth, and every tongue should confess that Jesus Christ is Lord, to the glory of God the Father.

Philippians 2:9-11

Jesus authorizes us and empowers us to act in His name. It's His power that backs up our authority. The devil has to bow to the Christ in us when we exercise our authority.

Think about the police officer whose directing traffic. His badge gives him the authority to make you stop. He lifts up his hand and you stop. He doesn't have the physical power in his body to make you stop. You stop because you recognize his authority to make you stop. You know if you don't stop when he says stop, you're illegal and you'll pay a price. The cop exercises his authority in reliance on the natural government that empowered him. We exercise our authority in reliance on the supernatural government—the kingdom of God—that empowers us.

Our authority is based on what Jesus accomplished. Our authority is not what we accomplish or how well we pray, or our feelings or moods. Our authority is not based on our own strength, might, or power. Zechariah 4:6 reveals, "Not by might nor by power, but by My Spirit, says the Lord of Hosts."

Our faith energizes and activates our authority. Jesus said, "These signs will accompany those who believe: In My name they will cast out demons; they will speak with new tongues; 18 they will take up serpents; if they drink any deadly thing, it will not hurt them; they will lay hands on the sick, and they will recover" (Mark 16:17-18).

God gave us dominion over the earth: We read about this in Genesis 1:26-28:

> *Then God said, "Let us make man in our image, after our likeness, and let them have dominion over the fish of the sea, and over the birds of the air, and over the livestock, and over all the earth, and over every creeping thing that creeps on the earth."*
>
> *So God created man in His own image; in the image of God He created him; male and female He created them. God blessed them and said to them, "Be fruitful and multiply, and replenish the earth and subdue it. Rule over the fish of the sea and over the birds of the air and over every living thing that moves on the earth."*

Psalm 115:16 tells us,

> *The heavens belong to the Lord, but the earth He has given to the children of men.*

Adam committed high treason and gave his authority over the earth to Satan. The good news is Jesus defeated Satan as the Son Man and took back all authority (see Colossians 2:15). He expects us to take authority in the earth and not cede our authority to the wicked one in any area of our lives, families, cities, or nations.

God gives us authority to resist and stand against the devil: Several scriptures make it clear that this is not only a right, but it's our responsibility as ambassadors for Jesus.

Ephesians 4:27 tells us directly, "Do not give place to the devil." The NASB says "do not leave room for the devil." The Message says, "Don't give the Devil that kind of foothold in your life." The Berean Literal Bible says, "Neither give opportunity to the devil." The International Standard Version tells us, "Do not give the devil an opportunity to work." The Aramaic Bible in Plain English warns us, "Neither should you give place to The Slanderer." That's pretty clear instruction.

Ephesians 6:13-14 tells us, "Therefore take up the whole armor of God that you may be able to resist in the evil day, and having done all, to stand." The AMPC translation makes the point more emphatically: "Therefore put on God's complete armor, that you may be able to resist and stand your ground on the evil day [of danger], and, having done all [the crisis demands], to stand [firmly in your place]." The NLT exhorts us to, "Stand your ground."

James 4:7 tells us, "Therefore submit yourselves to God. Resist the devil, and he will flee from you." This goes back to understanding your authority and submitting to authority. If you are not submitted to God's authority, the enemy knows this and has no obligation to flee.

1. We are seated in heaven in a place of authority: Ephesians 2:4-6 tells us: "But God, being rich in mercy, because of His great love with which He loved us, even when we were dead in sins, made us alive together with Christ (by grace you have been saved), and He raised us up and seated us together in the heavenly places in Christ Jesus, so that in the coming ages He might show the surpassing riches of His grace in kindness toward us in Christ Jesus."

2. The Spirit that raised Christ from the dead dwells in us: We're not just seated in heavenly places—far above all principalities and powers—God has also given us incomparably great power (see Ephesians 1:19). Indeed, the spirit that raised Christ from the dead dwells in us (see Romans 8:11). This positions us to have power over all the power of the enemy (see Luke 10:19).

3. We must actively exercise our authority or it's useless: Having authority alone is not enough. You can have a bank account full of money and still go hungry if you don't withdraw funds to buy food. The enemy will continue attacking us if we don't exercise our authority. 1 Peter 5:8-9 tells us, "Be sober and watchful, because your adversary the devil walks around as a roaring lion, seeking whom he may devour. Resist him firmly in the faith, knowing that the same afflictions are experienced by your brotherhood throughout the world."

4. We can't understand our authority with our mind alone. We need to pray for revelation in our spirit. You can pray this prayer: Father, in the name of Jesus, I ask You to give me a revelation of the authority Your Son delegated to me. God, open my eyes to the authority that abides in me, in the name of Jesus. Help me understand—to truly understand—the power with which you have endued me so that I can gain the confidence to run to the battle line like David and fight every battle on my path to the destiny you have in store for me, in Jesus' name.

5. God is waiting on us to take authority in the earth: Jesus said clearly, "I will give you the keys of the kingdom of heaven, and whatever you bind on earth shall be bound

in heaven, and whatever you loose on earth shall be loosed in heaven" (Matthew 16:19). The NLT puts it this way: "And I will give you the keys of the Kingdom of Heaven. Whatever you forbid on earth will be forbidden in heaven, and whatever you permit on earth will be permitted in heaven."

GOD's Word Translation says, "I will give you the keys of the kingdom of heaven. Whatever you imprison, God will imprison. And whatever you set free, God will set free." And the AMPC tells us, "I will give you the keys of the kingdom of heaven; and whatever you bind (declare to be improper and unlawful) on earth must be what is already bound in heaven; and whatever you loose (declare lawful) on earth must be what is already loosed in heaven."

MEDITATE ON YOUR AUTHORITY

Take the time to meditate—really think about these verses and take any advantage away from the wicked one.

These signs will accompany those who believe: In My name they will cast out demons; they will speak with new tongues; they will take up serpents; if they drink any deadly thing, it will not hurt them; they will lay hands on the sick, and they will recover.

Mark 16:17-18

I will give you the keys of the kingdom of heaven, and whatever you bind on earth shall be bound in heaven, and whatever you loose on earth shall be loosed in heaven.

Matthew 16:19

Truly, truly I say to you, he who believes in Me will do the works that I do also. And he will do greater works than these, because I am going to My Father.

John 14:12

For truly I say to you, whoever says to this mountain, "Be removed and be thrown into the sea," and does not doubt in his heart, but believes that what he says will come to pass, he will have whatever he says.

Mark 11:23

But you shall receive power when the Holy Spirit comes upon you. And you shall be My witnesses in Jerusalem, and in all Judea and Samaria, and to the ends of the earth.

Acts 1:8

And they cast out many demons and anointed with oil many who were sick and healed them.

Mark 6:13

The seventy returned with joy, saying, "Lord, even the demons are subject to us through Your name."

He said to them, "I saw Satan as lightning fall from heaven. Look, I give you authority to trample on serpents and scorpions, and over all the power of the enemy. And nothing shall by any means hurt you."

Luke 10:17-19

He called His twelve disciples to Him and gave them authority over unclean spirits, to cast them out, and to heal all kinds of sickness and all kinds of disease.

Matthew 10:1

You shall tread upon the lion and adder; the young lion and the serpent you shall trample underfoot.

Psalm 91:13

And to have authority to heal sicknesses and to cast out demons...

Mark 3:15

Heal the sick, cleanse the lepers, raise the dead, and cast out demons. Freely you have received, freely give.

Matthew 10:8

10

An Abominable Enemy

AFTER ATHALIAH ASCENDED TO THE THRONE through treachery, she was so confident in her legacy the megalomaniac seriously believed she was invincible. Apparently, she had a short-term memory. She forgot the fate of her mother, who was cast down by her own eunuchs, trampled by horses and the dogs ate her flesh (see 2 Kings 9:30-37). Perhaps she thought she was greater than her mother and with Jehu out of the picture she was without rival.

Athaliah was oblivious to the reality that the true successor, Jehoash, was waiting until God's perfect timing to take over the kingdom of Judah. God had a plan to strike Athaliah down before Athaliah ever ascended. As the proverb says, "Pride goes before destruction and a haughty spirit before a fall" (Proverbs 16:18). Proverbs 11:2 further emphasizes that disgrace follows pride and Proverbs 18:2 says a man's proud heart leads to a downfall.

Athaliah set up her family for a fall, never understanding that she was setting herself up for the ultimate fall. Because she walked continually in abominations, she provoked the Lord to deal with her swiftly. If Ahab provoked the Lord more than any other king, Athaliah certainly provoked the Lord more than any other queen.

Proverbs 6:16-19 reads, "These six things the Lord hates, Yes, seven are an abomination to Him: A proud look, a lying tongue, hands that shed innocent blood, a heart that devises wicked plans, feet that are swift in running to evil, a false witness who speaks lies, and one who sows discord among brethren." Athaliah walked in all of these and more abominations.

UNDERSTANDING ABOMINATIONS

What does abomination mean? Extreme disgust and hatred and loathing, according to *Merriam-Webster's dictionary*. Abomination is mentioned in the New King James Version of the Bible 144 times. Some of these mentions have to do with the Israelites being an abomination to their enemies, but many of these references have to do with things abominable to God.

Proverbs 3:32 says the perverse person is an abomination to the Lord while Proverbs 8:7 says wickedness is an abomination to the lips. Proverbs 11:1 reveals dishonest scales are an abomination and Proverbs 15:8 tells us the sacrifice of the wicked is an abomination. Even the thoughts of the wicked are an abomination, according to Proverbs 15:26. The list goes on and on. Athaliah was a walking, talking, ruling and reigning abomination.

ATHALIAH'S ABERRANT ABOMINATIONS

Proverbs 6 points out haughty eyes. Haughty eyes speak of someone with a prideful attitude that thinks they are better than other people. The definition of haughty is "blatantly and disdainfully proud, having or showing an attitude of superiority and contempt for people or things perceived to be inferior."

Satan is the Father of all lies, and some people let him get hold of their tongues without repentance. Proverbs 12:22 echoes Proverbs 6: "Lying lips are an abomination to the Lord, but those who deal truthfully are His delight." Athaliah was a liar and a usurper, just like her mother Jezebel.

The hands that shed innocent blood in Proverbs 6 are not relegated to actual murder, but also character assassination. People who slander and curse others behind the scenes are going to fall into their own net. Proverbs 15:26 speaks into this: "The thoughts of the wicked are an abomination to the Lord, but the words of the pure are pleasant." People cooperating with the spirit of Athaliah will assassinate your character, just like Jezebel.

Proverbs 16:5 echoes this: "Everyone proud in heart is an abomination to the Lord; Though they join forces, none will go unpunished." And again Proverbs 11:20 tells us: "Those who are of a perverse heart are an abomination to the Lord, but the blameless in their ways are His delight."

Feet that are swift in running to mischief are an abomination. The Message says, "feet that race down a wicked track." This is not accidental sin. This is executing the sin in a heart that devises wicked schemes. This is purposeful wickedness. A false witness who utters lies is an abomination. This is not just lying, but lying to bring others intentional harm. The Passion says, "sprouting lies in false testimony." Spreading strife is an abomination. Proverbs 24:9 echoes this: "The devising of foolishness is sin, And the scoffer is an abomination to men."

Like her parents Ahab and Jezebel, Athaliah was an idolator, serving false gods.

> *You shall burn the carved images of their gods with fire; you shall not covet the silver or gold that is on them, nor take it for yourselves, lest you be snared by it; for it is an abomination to the Lord your God. Nor shall you bring an abomination into your house, lest you be doomed to destruction like it. You shall utterly detest it and utterly abhor it, for it is an accursed thing.*

Deuteronomy 7:25-26

11

A Wicked
Counselor

IT'S NO ACCIDENT DAVID, a man after God's own heart, used the first verses in the first Psalm to offer some sage advice. It's wisdom that cautions us to be careful about the counsel we receive. While David surely didn't see Athaliah's day coming, especially since God promised the warrior king he would always have a descendent on the throne, he did understand that his son and his successors would need the wisdom in Psalm 1:1-3:

Blessed is the man
Who walks not in the counsel of the ungodly,
Nor stands in the path of sinners,
Nor sits in the seat of the scornful;
But his delight is in the law of the Lord,
And in His law he meditates day and night.
He shall be like a tree
Planted by the rivers of water,
That brings forth its fruit in its season,
Whose leaf also shall not wither;
And whatever he does shall prosper.

David pledged not to sit with deceitful or wicked men (see Psalm 26:4-5). Solomon gave ear to David's wisdom and offered similar wisdom of his own to guide his sons. Proverbs 12:15 reads, "The way of a fool is right in his own eyes, but he who heeds counsel is wise." And again in Proverbs 12:26,

"The righteous should choose his friends carefully, for the way of the wicked leads them astray."

ATHALIAH GIVES WICKED COUNSEL

Athaliah not only gives wicked counsel, but she's also a wicked counselor. We've already witnessed Athaliah has no fear of the Lord, and fear of the beginning of wisdom (see Proverbs 9:10). Not only does Athaliah lack a fear of the Lord and godly wisdom, but she also served false gods and followed her own demonic ambition. She possessed a wisdom, but not from God. We read about the type of wisdom Athaliah released in James 3:13-17 (AMPC).

Who is there among you who is wise and intelligent? Then let him by his noble living show forth his [good] works with the [unobtrusive] humility [which is the proper attribute] of true wisdom. But if you have bitter jealousy (envy) and contention (rivalry, selfish ambition) in your hearts, do not pride yourselves on it and thus be in defiance of and false to the Truth.

This [superficial] wisdom is not such as comes down from above, but is earthly, unspiritual (animal), even devilish (demoniacal). For wherever there is jealousy (envy) and contention (rivalry and selfish ambition), there will also be confusion (unrest, disharmony, rebellion) and all sorts of evil and vile practices.

But the wisdom from above is first of all pure (undefiled); then it is peace-loving, courteous (considerate, gentle). [It is willing to] yield to reason, full of compassion and good fruits; it is wholehearted and straightforward, impartial and unfeigned (free from doubts, wavering, and insincerity).

ATHALIAH ADVISES HER SON WICKEDLY

Here we see Athaliah's wisdom exposed. She had no good works, no humility, no true wisdom. Instead, she had bitter jealousy and envy, contention, rivalry, selfish ambition and the result in Judah was unrest, disharmony, rebellion, and all sorts of evil and vile practices—even killing her own grandchildren to clear a path to the throne for herself. We see Athaliah's wicked counsel and its outcome in 1 Chronicles 22:1-9:

> *Then those in Jerusalem made Ahaziah, the youngest son of Jehoram, king in his place because the raiding party, those coming with the Arabians to the camp, killed all the older sons. So Ahaziah the son of Jehoram reigned in Jerusalem. Now Ahaziah was forty-two years old when he began to reign, but he only reigned one year in Jerusalem. The name of his mother was Athaliah, a granddaughter of Omri.*
>
> *And he also walked in the ways of the house of Ahab because his mother was the one counseling him to do evil. And he also did what was evil in the eyes of the Lord, like the house of Ahab, for they served as his counselors after his father Jehoram died, which led to his destruction. Even Ahaziah walked in their counsel and went with Jehoram the son of Ahab king of Israel to war against Hazael king of Aram at Ramoth Gilead. And the Arameans wounded Joram, and the king returned to Jezreel to heal from the wounds that he sustained in Ramah where he fought against Hazael king of Aram.*
>
> *Then Ahaziah the son of Jehoram king of Judah went down to see Joram the son of Ahab in Jezreel because he was wounded.*

And it was from God that a downfall would happen to Ahaziah in regard to his visit with Joram. And when he arrived he went out with Joram to see Jehu the son of Nimshi, whom the Lord anointed to cut off the house of Ahab. And it happened that when Jehu was acting in judgment with the house of Ahab that he found the rulers of Judah and the sons of the brothers of Ahaziah, who were serving Ahaziah, and Jehu killed them. He sought out Ahaziah, and they captured him while he hid in Samaria, and they brought him to Jehu, and they put him to death. And they buried him because they said, "He is the grandson of Jehoshaphat who sought the Lord with all his heart." And there was no one from the house of Ahaziah strong enough to retain the kingdom.

And that's when Athaliah rose to power.

THE DANGER OF WICKED COUNSEL

You need to learn to discern between wise and wicked counsel. Athaliah can send people into your life with wicked counsel that defies the will of the Lord. Consider this passage in James 3:13-18:

Who is wise and understanding among you? Let him show by good conduct that his works are done in the meekness of wisdom. But if you have bitter envy and self-seeking in your hearts, do not boast and lie against the truth. This wisdom does not descend from above, but is earthly, sensual, demonic. For where envy and self-seeking exist, confusion and every evil thing are there. But the wisdom that is from above is first pure, then peaceable, gentle, willing to yield, full of mercy and good fruits, without partiality and without hypocrisy. Now the fruit of righteousness is sown in peace by those who make peace.

People who call themselves Christians can unintentionally give you wicked counsel. Be careful who you allow to speak into your life. When David was running from Saul, he had an opportunity to murder the king while he was asleep. His companions gave him wicked counsel, suggesting that he take the shot. These were people who were with and for David, but they did not have the counsel of the Lord. It was wicked counsel. Even a good person can give you wicked counsel. You have to discern.

Remember when Peter pulled Jesus aside and rebuked him? We see the account in Mark 8:31-33:

> *And He began to teach them that the Son of Man must suffer many things, and be rejected by the elders and chief priests and scribes, and be killed, and after three days rise again. He spoke this word openly. Then Peter took Him aside and began to rebuke Him. But when He had turned around and looked at His disciples, He rebuked Peter, saying, "Get behind Me, Satan! For you are not mindful of the things of God, but the things of men."*

Peter had just received one of the greatest revelations any man could claim directly from the throne room. Peter had discerned Jesus was the Christ, the Messiah. Moments later, this same Peter was influenced by another spirit. Jesus actually turned to Peter and said, "Get behind Me, Satan." Peter gave Jesus wicked counsel. Yet Peter was not wicked. Even a good person can give you wicked counsel. You have to discern.

Let me give you one more example to drive the point home. When Solomon died, Rehoboam took the throne. The people pledged to be loyal to him if they would just ease the heavy load Solomon put on them. Rehoboam sought counsel from the elders, who suggested he grant their requests. This was the wisdom of God. But Rehoboam didn't like what he heard so he asked his friends. Their advice, from 1 Kings 12:10-11

> *Thus you should speak to this people who have spoken to you, saying, "Your father made our yoke heavy, but you make it lighter on us"—thus you shall say to them: "My little finger shall be thicker than my father's waist! And now, whereas my father put a heavy yoke on you, I will add to your yoke; my father chastised you with whips, but I will chastise you with scourges!"*

Rehoboam followed the advice of his buddies. He took the wicked counsel. That decision caused him to lose favor and rulership over Israel. The people made Jeroboam king over Israel. Rehoboam only kept Judah and Benjamin in the end.

DISCERNING WICKED COUNSEL

You have to discern wicked counsel. Paul warned,

> *"See to it that no one carries you off as spoil or makes you yourselves captive by his so-called philosophy and intellectualism and vain deceit (idle fancies and plain nonsense), following human tradition (men's ideas of the material rather than the spiritual world), just crude notions following the rudimentary and elemental teachings of the universe and disregarding [the teachings of] Christ (the Messiah)"*

Colossians 2:8 (AMPC)

Wicked counsel may sound good at first, but consider the consequences before you act. Wicked counsel will not create peace, but confusion. And God is not the author of confusion but of peace (see 1 Corinthians 14:33). Wicked counsel taps into your fleshly impulses and desire for justice or even revenge. Wicked counsel defies the Word of God. Wicked counsel taps into your selfish ambition or greed.

Wicked counsel is not always easy to discern. Remember the serpent in the Garden? He gave Eve wicked counsel to eat the forbidden fruit, promising she would understand good and evil (see Genesis 3). Eve walked very closely with God in the Garden, and was still deceived by the enemy's crafty ways. Don't ever think you are above being deceived. Seek to discern godly versus wicked counsel, even if it comes from a trusted source.

Paul said, "But test and prove all things [until you can recognize] what is good; [to that] hold fast" (1 Thessalonians 5:21).

If you want to go deep on discernment, check out my intensive: *Developing Spiritual Discernment*. It can be found at schoolofthespirit.tv. And remember, Jesus is a Wonderful Counselor (see Isaiah 9:6).

12

Preparing to Annihilate Athaliah

YOU CAN'T JUST CONTEND WITH ATHALIAH, you have to annihilate the wicked works of this spirit in your life. Yes, I said annihilate. Yes, I know annihilate is a strong word. It means "to cause to cease to exist; to do away with entirely so that nothing remains; to defeat overwhelmingly; to cause to be of no effect; to destroy the substance or force of," according to *Merriam-Webster's dictionary*.

We have precedence for this. In 2 Kings 9:30-37, we see Jezebel's last stand and annihilation:

> *Now when Jehu had come to Jezreel, Jezebel heard of it; and she put paint on her eyes and adorned her head, and looked through a window. Then, as Jehu entered at the gate, she said, "Is it peace, Zimri, murderer of your master?"*
>
> *And he looked up at the window, and said, "Who is on my side? Who?" So two or three eunuchs looked out at him. Then he said, "Throw her down." So they threw her down, and some of her blood spattered on the wall and on the horses; and he trampled her underfoot. And when he had gone in, he ate and drank. Then he said, "Go now, see to this accursed woman, and bury her, for she was a king's daughter."*
>
> *So they went to bury her, but they found no more of her than the skull and the feet and the palms of her hands. Therefore they came back and told him. And he said, "This is the word*

of the Lord, which He spoke by His servant Elijah the Tishbite, saying, "On the plot of ground at Jezreel dogs shall eat the flesh of Jezebel; and the corpse of Jezebel shall be as refuse on the surface of the field, in the plot at Jezreel, so that they shall not say, "Here lies Jezebel."

PREPARING TO ANNIHILATE ATHALIAH

We know we will never completely eradicate Jezebel or Athaliah from the earth until Jesus comes back. But we can eradicate the works of these wayward spirits from our lives, our churches, our businesses and anywhere else the Lord has given us authority to steward—and God expects us not to tolerate Jezebel or Athaliah.

Before God brought the Israelites into the promised land, He gave them this instruction in Deuteronomy 7:1-2 (NET):

When the Lord your God brings you to the land that you are going to occupy and forces out many nations before you--Hittites, Girgashites, Amorites, Canaanites, Perizzites, Hivites, and Jebusites, seven nations more numerous and powerful than you—and he delivers them over to you and you attack them, you must utterly annihilate them. Make no treaty with them and show them no mercy!"

And the Lord reemphasized this in Deuteronomy 7:22-24 (BSB),

The Lord your God will drive out these nations before you little by little. You will not be enabled to eliminate them all at once, or the wild animals would multiply around you. But the Lord your God will give them over to you and throw them into great confusion, until they are destroyed. He will hand their kings over to you, and you will wipe out their names from under heaven. No one will be able to stand against you; you will annihilate them.

David understood the concept and the need for annihilation. He once said, "You have made my enemies retreat before me; I annihilate those who hate me" (2 Samuel 22:41, CSB). And again, "As a demonstration of your loyal love, destroy my enemies! Annihilate all who threaten my life, for I am your servant" (Psalm 143:12, NET). And again, "He will repay my adversaries for their evil. Because of your faithfulness, annihilate them" (Psalm 54:5, NET).

Remember, Athaliah is a spirit that annihilates. Keep in mind 2 Chronicles 22:10 (CSB), "When Athaliah, Ahaziah's mother, saw that her son was dead, she proceeded to annihilate all the royal heirs of the house of Judah. If you aren't prepared to annihilate all traces of Athaliah, you are in for long, hard seasons of battle with continued suffering.

DO NOT LET ONE GET AWAY

You'll remember when Saul spared King Agag after God told him through the prophet Samuel to "go and attack Amalek, and utterly destroy all that they have, and do not spare them. But kill both man and woman, infant and nursing child, ox and sheep, camel and donkey" (1 Kings 15:3). Saul went to battle and won, but did not follow through with the Lord's crystal clear instructions.

Samuel called the act of disobedience evil, and Saul lost his kingdom that day. "Samuel said to him, 'The Lord has torn the kingdom of Israel from you today, and has given it to a neighbor of yours, who is better than you. And also the

Strength of Israel will not lie nor relent. For He is not a man, that He should relent" (1 Samuel 15:28-29).

Understand this: Athaliah is after your kingdom—your domain. Athaliah wants to take over your home, your business, your church. This insidious spirit wants to usurp your God-given authority in your territory or realm of influence. If you don't annihilate the works of Athaliah—if you let one get away—you will continue paying a price you can't afford. I can't stress this enough.

That's why God continually told the Israelites: do not let one get away. In Numbers 33:55, God warned the Israelites, "But if you do not drive out the inhabitants of the land from before you, then those whom you let remain will be like thorns in your eyes and thorns in your sides. They will show hostility to you in the land in which you live."

While there is no "one and done" battle with Athaliah— we can expect her to come back at opportune times—we can determine ahead, during and after the attack to stand against this demon. We can stand and withstand with such fervent prayer that Athaliah will think twice—or maybe even three times—before continuing to rise and attack. While she's thinking, we're on the offense, armored up and ready to run.

DISASSOCIATING WITH ATHALIAH'S FOLLOWERS

Jehoiada understood if he did not rid Judah of Athaliah's followers, that same spirit in which she and her loyalists were operating would continue troubling the Jehoash's kingdom. In Athaliah's downfall, the priest also ordered the executioners to "slay with the sword however follows her" (2 Kings 11:15). The New Living Translation says, "anyone who tries to rescue her."

If you are associating with Athaliah's followers, Athaliah has proximity to your life and you are still holding some measure of agreement with this spirit. You will suffer the spiritual warfare consequences of aligning with Athaliah's followers—those sympathetic to Athaliah's cause and the witchcraft she releases. Practically speaking, that means people who carry the attributes we've discussed in this book or sympathizes with those who do.

Paul put it this way,

I meant that you are not to associate with anyone who claims to be a believer yet indulges in sexual sin, or is greedy, or worships idols, or is abusive, or is a drunkard, or cheats people. Don't even eat with such people.

1 Corinthians 5:11 (NLT)

And again,

And now, dear brothers and sisters, we give you this command in the name of our Lord Jesus Christ: Stay away from all believers who live idle lives and don't follow the tradition they received from us.

2 Thessalonians 3:5 (NLT)

We are responsible for the company we keep.

Jezebel's followers were the false prophets, Ahab, the eunuchs, and her spiritual children (those who learned from her and followed her leadership). Athaliah also gathers false prophets and teachers, so if you are sowing into and cheering on propagators of false prophecy and theology, the enemy not only has a right to infiltrate your mind with lies—he already has. I talk more about this in my book, Discerning Prophetic Witchcraft. If you are agreeing with darkness, you will pay a price.

Jesus meant what He said when He spoke of Jezebel and I believe the same applies to Athaliah and her followers:

And I gave her time to repent of her sexual immorality, and she did not repent. Indeed I will cast her into a sickbed, and those who commit adultery with her into great tribulation, unless they repent of their deeds. I will kill her children with death, and all the churches shall know that I am He who searches the minds and hearts. And I will give to each one of you according to your works.

Revelation 2:21-23

This is a scary passage and one we need to take seriously. If we are tolerating Athaliah, Jesus has something against us. If we are in bed with Athaliah, we need to repent.

REPENTANCE: A PREREQUISITE

We can get so strong in our spirits and so sensitive to God that we discern Athaliah coming from miles away and raise up a standard against her. That starts with repentance. Before you go into any battle, repentance is the prerequisite. A prerequisite is something that is both required and necessary to carry out a function or objective. Remember when you were in college, you had had to take Class 101 before you could take Class 102. There were prerequisites. Throughout the pages of this book, I have exhorted you to examine your heart and look for common ground. Now is the time to repent. As I wrote in my book, *101 Tactics for Spiritual Warfare*:

If you are practicing sin, you won't successfully maintain victory over the enemy. We see this principle under Joshua's leadership when Achan violated the word of the Lord, took some of the spoils of war and hid them underground in his tent. His sin opened a door to great casualties in its next battle (see Joshua 7).

From this account, we learn the principle of repenting before going into battle. Never enter into warfare without first entering into repentance for personal sin.

> *Who may ascend the mountain of the Lord? Who may stand in his holy place? The one who has clean hands and a pure heart, who does not trust in an idol or swear by a false god. He will receive the blessing from the Lord, and vindication from God their Savior.*
>
> Psalm 24:3–5 (NIV)

> *He who covers his sins will not prosper, but whoever confesses and forsakes them will have mercy.*
>
> Proverbs 28:13

When John the Baptist preached, "Repent, for the kingdom of heaven is at hand!" (Matthew 3:2) that word repent came from the Greek word *metanoeo*. *Metanoeo* means "to change one's mind, i.e., to repent; to change one's mind for the better, heartily to amend with abhorrence of one's past sins."

True repentance means a change of heart about the sin you've committed—seeing it the way God sees it, renouncing it, and turning away from it. Paul the apostle breaks it down scripturally and contrasts worldly sorrow with godly sorrow in a powerful way in 2 Corinthians 7:8–12 (NKJV):

> *For even if I made you sorry with my letter, I do not regret it; though I did regret it. For I perceive that the same epistle made you sorry, though only for a while. Now I rejoice, not that you were made sorry, but that your sorrow led to*

repentance. For you were made sorry in a godly manner, that you might suffer loss from us in nothing. For godly sorrow produces repentance leading to salvation, not to be regretted; but the sorrow of the world produces death. For observe this very thing, that you sorrowed in a godly manner: What diligence it produced in you, what clearing of yourselves, what indignation, what fear, what vehement desire, what zeal, what vindication! In all things you proved yourselves to be clear in this matter. Therefore, although I wrote to you, I did not do it for the sake of him who had done the wrong, nor for the sake of him who suffered wrong, but that our care for you in the sight of God might appear to you.

Don't let this call to repentance offend you. Heed the warning and the good news of John, the apostle of love, in 1 John 1:5–10:

This is the message which we have heard from Him and declare to you, that God is light and in Him is no darkness at all. If we say that we have fellowship with Him, and walk in darkness, we lie and do not practice the truth. But if we walk in the light as He is in the light, we have fellowship with one another, and the blood of Jesus Christ His Son cleanses us from all sin.

If we say that we have no sin, we deceive ourselves, and the truth is not in us. If we confess our sins, He is faithful and just to forgive us our sins and to cleanse us from all unrighteousness. If we say that we have not sinned, we make Him a liar, and His word is not in us.

We all fall short of the glory of God every day. Repentance itself can cause the warfare to stop because we are resisting him and submitting ourselves to God. When we do this, according to James 4:7 he has to flee.

13

Call In
the Executioners

DEFEATING ATHALIAH REQUIRES supernatural backup. We can't go toe to toe with principalities—or even garden variety demons—in our own strength. We need the mighty weapons of God, the whole armor of God, other spiritual warriors to stand with us, and sometimes the host of heaven to join in the battle.

Jehoiada, a high priest in Judah, knew dethroning Athaliah meant calling in the executioners who were experienced in dealing with treacherous enemies of God. Those executioners in Bible days were known as the Carites. 2 Kings 11:4 (NLT) records,

> *In the seventh year of Athaliah's reign, Jehoiada the priest summoned the commanders, the Carite mercenaries, and the palace guards to come to the Temple of the Lord.*

First, note that this plan to overthrow Athaliah was hatched on the seventh year. Why wait so long? Why let this ruthless murderess reign for six years? It could be possible the people of Judah finally said, "Enough is enough." We don't know what life was like under Athaliah's tyranny, but the priest was clearly grieved. It could be they were waiting for the true heir to the throne to mature to an age where he could rule Judah.

Pulpit Commentary writes,

After waiting, impatiently we may be sure, for six long years, and seeing the young prince grow from an infant to a boy of seven years of age, Jehoiada deemed that the time was come to venture on an effort. It was necessary for him to make his arrangements beforehand with great care. His first step was to sound the captains of the royal guard.

One thing is sure: It was the timing of the Lord to end Athaliah's tyranny.

WHO ARE THE CARITES?

Why did the priest call in Carites? Who are these Carites? *Carite* means executioner. The New Living Translation uses the word mercenary. When you think of mercenaries, you may think of Rambo, the character Sylvester Stallone played in the movie series by the same name. Mercenaries are executioners who work for pay.

Some say the Carites were actually the former king's own bodyguards. (Athaliah probably had her own guard loyal to her interests just as Jezebel had false prophets eating at her table.) Others say the Carites were officers commanding the royal guard. Either way, can you imagine having Rambo as a bodyguard? And there was more than one! The priest wasn't taking any chances on losing to Athaliah. He knew this wicked woman, though demonized, was no match for the mercenaries.

Some commentaries say the Carites, or as they are also called the Cherethites, were a group of elite mercenaries King David himself employed. As such, they would not be loyal to

Athaliah but to the seed of David and would be aware of the promise God made to David that He would establish his throne forever (see 2 Samuel 20:12-16). Just as David when he faced Goliath, the Carites had a worthy cause at hand.

JEHOIADA COMMISSIONS THE MERCENARIES

The wise priest didn't just call the Carites to the house of the Lord, He called them to covenant to overthrow Athaliah. After Jehoiada made a covenant with these mercenaries, he put them under oath in the house of the Lord not to reveal the prince. Only then did he show them the king's son. Doubtless, he swore them to secrecy.

Imagine the shock when the Carites discovered the true heir was alive. Keep in mind at this point, only a handful of people knew the boy prince Jehoash had been preserved in the midst of his grandmother Athaliah's serial murders. Read the account in 2 Kings 11:5 (AMP): "Then he made a covenant with them and put them under oath in the house of the Lord, and showed them the king's [hidden] son."

The *Jamieson-Fausset-Brown Bible Commentary* reports:

The conduct of Jehoiada, who acted the leading and chief part in this conspiracy, admits of an easy and full justification; for, while Athaliah was a usurper, and belonged to a race destined by divine denunciation to destruction, even his own wife had a better and stronger claim to the throne; the sovereignty of Judah had been divinely appropriated to the family of David, and therefore the young prince on whom it was proposed to confer the crown, possessed an inherent right to it, of which a usurper could not deprive him.

WHO ARE TODAY'S CARITES?

Today's Carites are not a special breed of prayer warriors. Rather, the Carites represent angels of judgment released against the spirit of Athaliah. As I write in *Angels on Assignment Again*, God sends angels of judgment, or execution angels, to do His bidding at times.

We see this over and again in Scripture. Psalm 78:9 speaks of a band of destroying angels. We know angels of judgment visited Sodom and Gomorrah before fire and brimstone destroyed the ancient cities (see Genesis 19:13). In 2 Kings 19:35, we read,

> *And it came to pass on a certain night that the angel of the Lord went out, and killed in the camp of the Assyrians one hundred and eighty-five thousand; and when people arose early in the morning, there were the corpses—all dead.*

David saw the angels of judgment after he sinned in taking a census of his kingdom. 1 Chronicles 21:15-16 reads,

> *And God sent an angel to Jerusalem to destroy it. As he was destroying, the Lord looked and relented of the disaster, and said to the angel who was destroying, "It is enough; now restrain your hand."*
>
> *And the angel of the Lord stood by the threshing floor of Ornan the Jebusite. Then David lifted his eyes and saw the angel of the Lord standing between earth and heaven, having in his hand a drawn sword stretched out over Jerusalem. So David and the elders, clothed in sackcloth, fell on their faces.*

When dealing with Athaliah, we need to release the angels of judgment, the execution angels—the Carites. Notice, the priest ordered the execution, but he did not perform it. We can wield the weapons of war to fight the good fight of faith against this tyrannical spirit, but ultimately it's the power of God that brings down Athaliah. We are enforcing a victory God already won, and relying on the heavenly host to help enforce that victory on earth as it is in heaven.

14

Divine Downloads of Destruction

DO NOT LET ONE GET AWAY, but get a divine download of destruction from the Lord. That's what Jehoiada did. Calling in the mercenaries and making a covenant with them was part of that divine strategy. But that's just where it started.

Jehoiada was a priest—many scholars say he was the high priest—but he was not a warrior. Still, he had wisdom in war. He was able to tap into the mind of God. While David once asked, "Shall I go up?" Jehoiada may have asked, "How do I go up?" The strategy may be different every time, though the overarching principles are the same.

Noteworthy is the fact that the name Jehoiada means "the Lord knows." Doubtless, the priest did not know what to do when Athaliah seized the throne, but he prayed about it. He sought the Lord. He probably fasted. And, ultimately, he did what he knew to do at the time: keep the prince Jehoash safe. Can you imagine hiding a small child all those years?

Jehoiada held out hope and faith that Lord would show him what to do when he needed to do it. At the right time, he secured a divine strategy from the Lord. The Lord knows how to defeat the Athaliah attack in your life—and it's not the same for every battle.

JEHOIADA'S DIVINE STRATEGY

Jehoiada's divine strategy included guards, watchmen and warriors to guard against the Athaliah attack on the would-be boy king. Let's look at little closer. After he called in the mercenaries and showed them the king's son,

> *He commanded them, saying, "This is what you shall do: One-third of you who come on duty on the Sabbath shall be keeping watch over the king's house, one-third shall be at the gate of Sur, and one-third at the gate behind the escorts. You shall keep the watch of the house, lest it be broken down,"*

2 Kings 11:6

The Hebrew word guard in this verse is *mishmereth*. The word means to guard, watch, keep, or preserve in the sense of defense. Depending on the attack, sometimes you have to put up your defense before you go on the offense. In other words, if Athaliah has already wreaked havoc on your life, you need to stop the bleeding before you can head back to the battlefield. Don't charge forward with a limp if you don't have to. Reassess and repair the breaches before you attempt to strike Athaliah down.

And know this: You can't just bind this demon. You have to dethrone it from the place in your life where it has settled, either out of ignorance, complacency or agreement. You can't just throw it down like the eunuchs threw Jezebel out of her high window. You have to evict Athaliah forcibly from any place of authority or influence in your life. You have to cut it off. You have to strike her down.

Now, you may have heard me say, "You can't break the Jezebel assignment until you break the Jezebel alignment." That means if you have people in close proximity to you—if you are in close relationship with someone who has a Jezebelic spirit and you are tolerating it—you can't break the assignment. You get what you tolerate. Jesus told us not to tolerate Jezebel (see Revelation 2:20). It's the same with Athaliah. Part of your assignment is assessing where you have allowed Athaliah to operate and repent—changing the way you think.

If you are tolerating power-hungry character assassins who are narcissistic and the like—if you are putting up with behaviors in people that match Athaliah's modus operandi—you will not be able to overcome this spirit because you have an agreement with it, even if you hate it. You are permitting it to operate. You are allowing it to wreak havoc in your life. Sometimes you have to confront people operating in these spirits or close the door to them. Always allow the Holy Spirit to lead you.

GUARDING AGAINST ATHALIAH'S AMBUSH

The next step in Jehoiada's divine strategy is outlined in 2 Kings 11:7-8:

> *Two of your companies from all who go out on the Sabbath will keep watch over the house of the Lord for the king. You will encircle the king, each man with his weapons in his hand, and the one that comes within the ranks must be killed. They must be with the king when he goes out and comes in.*

In this context, a guard is one assigned to protect against a surprise attack. Catch that: Athaliah goes for the ambush. Think about it for a minute. A surprise attack is how she took the throne in the first place. Her relatives probably never saw the hit on their lives coming, especially her grandbabies. They never thought Grandma Attie would harm a hair on their heads. It was shock and awe in Judah.

Athaliah may catch you by surprise because it may operate through someone you know and trust—someone with whom you feel safe. Both Jezebel and Athaliah work through information seeking devices, creating soul ties and working to establish some level of intimacy with the victims before going in for the kill. Athaliah is an ambusher. She doesn't announce her plan like the queen mother Jezebel did when she sent a messenger to Elijah vowing to murder him within 24 hours. Athaliah kept her plots to herself. She's like a groundhog that stays underground until the right season.

This is how the enemy typically works. Paul warned,

Be well balanced (temperate, sober of mind), be vigilant and cautious at all times; for that enemy of yours, the devil, roams around like a lion roaring [in fierce hunger], seeking someone to seize upon and devour. Withstand him; be firm in faith [against his onset—rooted, established, strong, immovable, and determined], knowing that the same (identical) sufferings are appointed to your brotherhood (the whole body of Christians) throughout the world).

1 Peter 5:8-9 (AMPC)

ATHALIAH'S AUTHORITARIAN MINDSET

David wrote about the wicked man in Psalm 10, but this passage could just as easily describe Athaliah. Indeed, it describes Athaliah's mindset. Read Psalm 10:4-11 (AMPC):

The wicked one in the pride of his countenance will not seek, inquire for, and yearn for God; all his thoughts are that there is no God [so He never punishes]. His ways are grievous [or persist] at all times; Your judgments [Lord] are far above and on high out of his sight [so he never thinks about them]; as for all his foes, he sniffs and sneers at them.

He thinks in his heart, I shall not be moved; for throughout all generations I shall not come to want or be in adversity. His mouth is full of cursing, deceit, oppression (fraud); under his tongue are trouble and sin (mischief and iniquity).

He sits in ambush in the villages; in hiding places he slays the innocent; he watches stealthily for the poor (the helpless and unfortunate). He lurks in secret places like a lion in his thicket; he lies in wait that he may seize the poor (the helpless and the unfortunate); he seizes the poor when he draws him into his net.

[The prey] is crushed, sinks down; and the helpless falls by his mighty [claws]. [The foe] thinks in his heart, God has quite forgotten; He has hidden His face; He will never see [my deed].

ORCHESTRATING A TEAM EFFORT

Part of Jehoiada's strategy was to assemble a team. Typically, you need to assemble a crack team of spiritual warriors to combat Athaliah because make no mistake, Athaliah is not working alone. Athaliah has a fine-tuned, well-oiled, orchestrated team with thousands of years of experience on her side. And her team is merciless.

Jezebel, Ahab, witchcraft, python, and other spirits may be on her attack squad. And Athaliah is usually not just coming against your life, but your whole family or ministry or business. Athaliah comes with a multi-pronged attack. It's a corporate attack and needs a corporate response that includes guards, watchmen and warriors to discern and combat the Athaliah attack. You don't need all hands-on deck, but you do need Gideon's Army—those who are not afraid to fight.

Let's take a closer look at your strike team. When you come against Athaliah, you watchmen and warriors. You need prophetic guards who can see in the spirit so you can ready against the retaliation that's surely coming. Surround yourself with warriors. Make no mistake. When you set out to cast her down, this spirit will look to get to you first, attacking what's precious to you. Remember, Jehu didn't even defeat Jezebel alone. He partnered with the eunuchs to see her utter demise.

With spiritual warfare endeavors, there is strength in numbers. We know the Lord told Joshua:

One man of you shall chase a thousand, for the Lord your God is He who fights for you, as He promised you

Joshua 23:10

Those are pretty good odds, but it gets better with the multiplier effect. Deuteronomy 32:20 tells us two can put ten thousand to flight. And Deuteronomy 28:7 tells us when our enemy comes at us one way, he will flee seven ways.

Pushing back Athaliah's witchcraft is almost always a team effort. Jehoiada knew that, and he assembled an expert team of mercenaries and others to lead the charge. Although David defeated Goliath alone and Paul wrestled the beast at Ephesus all by himself, this level of warfare requires a coordinated effort against the ambush—and the retaliation. Yes, Samson and even some of David's mighty men fought alone at times, but God usually sends out warriors in teams. Leviticus 26:8 reiterates,

Five of you shall chase a hundred, and a hundred of you shall put ten thousand to flight; your enemies shall fall by the sword before you.

Jehoiada instructed in 1 Kings 11:5-9:

One-third of you who come on duty on the Sabbath shall be keeping watch over the king's house, one-third shall be at the gate of Sur, and one-third at the gate behind the escorts. You shall keep the watch of the house, lest it be broken down. The two contingents of you who go off duty on the Sabbath shall keep the watch of the house of the Lord for the king.

But you shall surround the king on all sides, every man with his weapons in his hand; and whoever comes within range, let him be put to death. You are to be with the king as he goes out and as he comes in. So the captains of the hundreds did according to all that Jehoiada the priest commanded. Each of them took his men who were to be on duty on the Sabbath, with those who were going off duty on the Sabbath, and came to Jehoiada the priest.

That said, don't be discouraged or feel helpless if you don't have a team. The Father, Son, and Holy Spirit will be your team. The angel armies will back you up. The battle ultimately belongs to the Lord (see 1 Samuel 17:47). It was this truth that fueled David's trust in his covenant with God that gave him the courage to battle Goliath. Deuteronomy 3:22 ensures,

You must not fear them, for the Lord your God Himself fights for you." And again, "For the Lord your God is He who goes with you, to fight for you against your enemies, to save you."

15

Brace for False Accusations

WHEN QUEEN JEZEBEL SAW the writing on the wall, she thought she could seduce, lie, and intimidate her way out of her fate. Jezebel thought she could manipulate her way into Jehu's good favor. She thought she could control the outcome of the encounter. Well, she thought wrong. And as we'll see in the pages ahead, Athaliah's insanity caused her to think she could play the same game and get a different result.

Consider the encounter between Jehu and Jezebel: "When Jehu came to Jezreel, Jezebel heard about it. She put black paint on her eyes, adorned her head, and looked down through the window. As Jehu entered in at the gate, she said, "Is everything all right, Zimri, murderer of his master?" (2 Kings 9:30–31). In her arrogance, Jezebel was waiting for Jehu and thought her plot to win him would work.

Jezebel painted her face and adorned her head—she was trying to seduce Jehu as she looked down on him through the window if perchance he might fall into her trap and make her his again. I wrote more about this in my book, *Jezebel's Puppets*. These were probably some of the tactics she used with Ahab. Remember, the devil has no new tricks. He usually doesn't need any because many Christians keep falling for the same maneuvers.

Now watch this. When Jezebel's strategy failed, she made false accusations against Jehu, comparing him to Zimri. You might wonder, who's Zimri? Zimri was the fifth king of

Israel, but he acquired his kingship through an insurrection. 1 Kings 16:8-10 reads:

> *In the twenty-sixth year of Asa king of Judah, Elah the son of Baasha became king over Israel, and reigned two years in Tirzah. Now his servant Zimri, commander of half his chariots, conspired against him as he was in Tirzah drinking himself drunk in the house of Arza, steward of his house in Tirzah. And Zimri went in and struck him and killed him in the twenty-seventh year of Asa king of Judah, and reigned in his place.*

But this accusation was actually laced in a curse. 1 Kings 16:15 tells us Zimri only ruled for seven days. That's one week. The people rebelled and made Omri—Ahab's father—king of Israel. Omri led the Israelites up to Tirzah to confront Zimri and what happens next is shocking:

> *And it happened, when Zimri saw that the city was taken, that he went into the citadel of the king's house and burned the king's house down upon himself with fire, and died.*

1 Kings 20:18

Zimri later committed suicide. Jezebel made a false accusation against Jehu, but she also released a death curse. By comparing him to Zimri, she was essentially saying, "Even if you do succeed in throwing me down, you will find yourself dead in a week." This was Jezebel hiding a threat in an accusation: "Jehu, coming against me is suicide."

This is similar to the curse Jezebel released against Elijah when she sent this message to the prophet: "So may the gods do to me and more also, if I do not make your life as the life of one of them by this time tomorrow" (I Kings 9:2). Though it took longer than a day, that curse boomeranged back to Jezebel in the Jehu moment.

ATHALIAH'S INSANITY

Athaliah may have been watching in the wings as her mother tried to work her witchcraft on Jehu. Although it clearly did not work—Jehu called for the eunuchs to throw her down and they did—Athaliah employed a similar tactic when she faced her executioner. When she discovered Jehoash was crowned, she took a page from her mother's playbook. That's why I called it insanity.

Although the quote didn't originate with Albert Einstein, we know he was prone to point out that the definition of insanity is doing the same thing over and over again and expecting a different result. Demonized, Athaliah was truly insane but her defense of insanity would not hold up in any court of law—especially God's court.

Here's the scene: Athaliah had just lost the throne as one of the king's sons, Jehoash, who survived her slaughter was anointed and crowned king. 2 Kings 11:13-14:

Now when Athaliah heard the noise of the escorts and the people, she came to the people in the temple of the Lord. When she looked, there was the king standing by a pillar according to custom; and the leaders and the trumpeters were by the king. All the people of the land were rejoicing and blowing trumpets.

What a shocking moment of defeat for the wicked queen. The ambusher was ambushed. The spoiler was spoiled, but she was too proud to admit defeat so she resorted to accusations that aimed to discredit the coronation of the boy king. 2 Kings 11:14 continues:

> *So Athaliah tore her clothes and cried out, "Treason! Treason!" And Jehoiada the priest commanded the captains of the hundreds, the officers of the army, and said to them, "Take her outside under guard, and slay with the sword whoever follows her." For the priest had said, "Do not let her be killed in the house of the Lord."*

Can you see the similarity? Just as Jezebel accused Jehu of treason, Athaliah accused the officers of the army of treason. Just as Jehu the king called for the eunuchs to throw down Jezebel, Jehoiada, the king's priest, called for the officers to strike down Athaliah.

ATHALIAH'S SLANDEROUS DEFENSE

Athaliah is a slanderer. Slander is not pretty. It means "to defame someone; to harm their reputation; to disgrace; or to accuse." Slander is a tool of the accuser of the brethren (see Revelation 12:10). Consider this: the word slanderer in 1 Timothy 3:11 is the same word for "devil." When we slander someone, we are acting like devils. We are mirroring the character of Satan. We can't walk in the anointing God has for us and mirror the character of Satan at the same time. We just can't.

Athaliah can manifest through people to slander you. No one likes to be slandered. I don't enjoy it. It makes me sorrow for the one who's committing the sin. The Bible says, "Whoever secretly slanders his neighbor, Him I will destroy" (Psalm 101:5, NKJV). And Romans 1:30-32 suggests backbiters are worthy of death. Paul told us not to keep company with a believer who has "a foul tongue [railing,

abusing, reviling, slandering]" (1 Corinthians 5:11, AMP)—
Scripture actually lists the slanderer among the sexually
immoral, the covetous, idolaters, drunkards and extortioners.
The point is, God hates slander. Can you see why we need to
pray for those who persecute us?

How you respond to mistreatment—even from demon
forces through vain imaginations that hit your mind—is one
of the most important aspects of your spiritual life. When we
respond the right way, we climb higher—or go deeper—in
the Spirit. When we respond the wrong way, we get bitter.
Over time, that bitterness will defile our spirits and dull our
ability to sense the presence of God or hear His voice.
Bitterness is deadly—and it's easy for the people around you
to discern. Where true humility lives, though, bitterness can't
take up residence. You don't want to become like the demon
you are fighting. Don't let Athaliah make you bitter.

GOD WILL VINDICATE YOU

I take heart in this passage from the Sermon on the
Mount:

> *Blessed are you when men revile you, and persecute you, and
> say all kinds of evil against you falsely for My sake. Rejoice
> and be very glad, because great is your reward in heaven, for
> in this manner they persecuted the prophets who were before
> you.*

Matthew 5:11-12

If Athaliah is persecuting you, know that God has a great
plan for you.

God is the judge. He will make the wrong things right in
His way and in His timing. Vengeance is His. He will repay

(see Romans 12:19). I won't be overcome with evil, but I will overcome evil with good (v. 21). I will rejoice when I am persecuted because I know that when I respond the right way, I am blessed. My first response is to pray for those who persecute me. And pray. And pray. And pray some more. It keeps my heart clean. I encourage you to do the same.

You need to let God vindicate you from Athaliah's attacks. Vindication is the story of my life. Time doesn't permit me to share all the details of the wrongs I've endured. But God is a vindicator. Our job is to hold out faith and keep our hearts right. In my devotional, *Mornings With the Holy Spirit*, I share these words God spoke to my heart in a past season:

> Don't seek to protect yourself. Father is your Protector. Love seeks not its own. I know it's difficult not to speak up or act out when people are trampling on your perceived rights. But a humble spirit gives up what it deserves. Humility does not fight for its rights. Take your cue from Jesus, who laid down everything that belonged to Him for your sake. Father vindicated Him and blessed Him with more than He gave away. Father will vindicate you in the same way—but you have to get out of His way. Seek the path of humility, and you will find what you really want.

Arguing with someone who has an Athaliah spirit isn't going to get you anywhere. And Athaliah can't pay you back for the attack. God will vindicate and repay. If you handle the attack right, you'll be more blessed after the dust settles than you were when the enemy kicked that dust into your face. Let these 12 vindication promises strengthen you to wait on the Lord to take vengeance upon your spiritual enemies.

YOUR WEAPONS OF VINDICATION

Here's the good news: God is no respecter of persons (Acts 10:34). If He will vindicate me, He will vindicate you. If He will restore what the devil stole from me, He will restore what the devil stole from you. So I challenge you right now, instead of complaining day and night about what the enemy has done in your life, try praying day and night for God's justice. Are you desperate enough for God's justice in your life that you'll persist in day and night prayer until you see Him move?

> *Shall God not avenge His own elect who cry out day and night to Him, though He bears long with them? I tell you that He will avenge them speedily. Nevertheless, when the Son of Man comes, will He really find faith on the earth?*

Luke 18:7-8

Do you believe that God is your vindicator? Is anything too hard for God? (see Jeremiah 32:26-27).

I don't know what Athaliah has done to malign you, who has done you wrong in the name of Athaliah, or what Athaliah has stolen from you. But what I am absolutely confident of is that God is your vindicator. If you believe it, and you persist in prayer for justice, day and night, you can assure someone else of our just God's vindicating power too. Only believe. Amen.

Your weapons of vindication are found in the Word. You can stand on God's Word to vindicate you. If He ever vindicated anybody, He will vindicate you. Put these weapons in your war chest. Let them build your faith. Speak these Scriptures out of your mouth.

***

Rachel said, "God has vindicated me, and He has also heard my voice and has given me a son." Therefore she called his name Dan.

Genesis 30:6 (MEV)

Judge me, O Lord,
for I have walked in my integrity.
I have trusted in the Lord;
I will not slip.

Psalm 26:1 (MEV)

Vindicate me, O God,
and plead my cause against an ungodly nation;
deliver me from the deceitful and unjust man.

Psalm 43:1 (MEV)

O God, save me by Your name,
and judge me by Your strength.

Psalm 54:1 (MEV)

He who vindicates Me is near;
Who will contend with Me?
Let us stand up to each other.
Who is my adversary?
Let him come near to me.

Isaiah 50:8 (MEV)

·Behold now, I have prepared my case;
I know that I will be vindicated.

Job 13:18 (NASB)

For the Lord will judge His people
And have compassion on His servants,
When He sees that their power is gone,
And there is no one remaining, bond or free.

Deuteronomy 32:36

The Lord has revealed our righteousness. Come and let us
declare in Zion the work of the Lord our God.

Jeremiah 51:10

He will bring forth your righteousness as the light,
and your judgment as the noonday.

Psalm 37:6 (MEV)

For You have maintained my right and my cause;
You sat on the throne judging righteously.

Psalm 9:4

May those shout for joy and rejoice,
who take delight in my vindication;
And may they say continually, "The Lord be exalted,
Who delights in the prosperity of His servant."

Psalm 35:27 (NASB)

16

Athaliah Always
Over Plays Her Hand

KEEP IN MIND THE DEVIL—including Athaliah—always overplays his hand. Always. That's what happened when I was in Singapore, struggling to tape those episodes about Jezebel for viewing in the nations only to later visit one of the TV staff's room and identify herself. Let me give you a real life example.

When I listened to my voicemail I was absolutely shocked. An angry young man on the other end of the line spewed, "How dare you, Jennifer LeClaire, tell Michael you don't believe me. Don't you know that I get every message you send and receive on your phone? How dare you!"

Yes, apparently someone I know found a way to hack into my smartphone's messaging system and intercept every text message I sent or received. This person was reading personal details about my life, as well as the lives of those I was ministering to, for months. It was beyond creepy.

Of course, when I realized this, I immediately signed out of my messaging account and changed all my passwords. But when the dust settled, I was reminded of a lesson: the devil always overplays his hand and, ultimately, the devil always exposes himself in the end. Although there's no scripture and verse in the Bible that says that, there are plenty of examples in the Word that prove the point.

JUSTIFYING JOB

Job's faith was sorely tested at the hand of Satan. Job lost his sons and daughters, his possessions, and even his health. It was so bad that his embittered wife suggested he curse God and die and his friends suggested there was some secret sin in his life. But he would not turn his back on Jehovah.

When He has tested me, I shall come forth as gold. My foot has held fast to His steps; I have kept His way and not turned aside. I have not departed from the commandment of His lips; I have treasured the words of His mouth, more than my necessary food.

Job 23:11-12

Although God gave Satan permission to sift Job, he overplayed his hand. God not only vindicated Job among his wife, brothers, sisters, and friends who judged his heart, he also set Job up as their intercessor, elevating him to a position of honor.

Job had a heart tender before God even in the face of the enemy's attacks. And we know the end of the story:

And the Lord restored Job's losses when he prayed for his friends. Indeed, the Lord gave Job twice as much as he had before

Job 42:10

MOSES MARCHED ON

Pharaoh kept the Israelites in bondage for hundreds of years. One day, God called a deliverer named Moses to tell Pharaoh, "Thus says the Lord God of Israel; 'Let My people go, that they may hold a feast to Me in the wilderness'" (Exodus 5:1). Pharaoh didn't take too kindly to that

126

command and made things even harder for the Israelites, commanding the taskmasters to withhold the straw to make bricks without reducing the quota of bricks (see Exodus 5:6:9).

After each plague God released into Egypt, Pharaoh would promise to let Israel go—and then change his mind. This happened over and over and over again until finally, one last time, Pharaoh actually allowed Israel to start leaving. But before they got too far out, Pharaoh changed his mind again and sent his army out against them. Pharaoh overplayed his hand and was defeated at the Red Sea.

> *Moses stretched out his hand over the sea; and when the morning appeared, the sea returned to its full depth, while the Egyptians were fleeing into it. So the Lord overthrew the Egyptians in the midst of the sea. Then the waters returned and covered the chariots, the horsemen, and all the army of Pharaoh that came into the sea after them. Not so much as one of them remained. But the children of Israel had walked on dry land in the midst of the sea, and the waters were a wall to them on their right hand and on their left.*

> Exodus 14:27-29

HAMAN FIGURATIVELY HANGED HIMSELF

Haman had it out for the Jews. He was second in command to the king. Everyone honored him except Mordecai, who refused to bow to him in the streets. Haman loathed Mordecai and when he discovered his Jewish descent he set in motion a plan to destroy not only Mordecai—but all the Jews. Form Esther 3:7-9:

Haman said to King Ahasuerus, "There is a certain people scattered and dispersed among the people in all the provinces of your kingdom; their laws are different from all other people's, and they do not keep the king's laws. Therefore it is not fitting for the king to let them remain. If it pleases the king, let a decree be written that they be destroyed, and I will pay ten thousand talents of silver into the hands of those who do the work, to bring it into the king's treasuries."

Mordecai called a fast and his niece, Esther—who happened to be married to the king—joined in. She found favor with the king, exposed Haman's plan, and turned it around on him.

The king said to Queen Esther, "The Jews have killed and destroyed five hundred men in Shushan the citadel, and the ten sons of Haman. What have they done in the rest of the king's provinces? Now what is your petition? It shall be granted to you. Or what is your further request? It shall be done." Esther said, "If it pleases the king, let it be granted to the Jews who are in Shushan to do again tomorrow according to today's decree, and let Haman's ten sons be hanged on the gallows."

Esther 9:12-13

Here's the takeaway: Be encouraged. The enemy sometimes turns up the heat, but God is in control. He won't allow more to come on you than you can bear—and he won't let the enemy have his way in the end. The devil always overplays his hand and God always restores anything Satan manages to kill, steal or destroy.

If you've lost anything at the enemy's hand, then believe for a Job-like restoration and if things look all but lost, remember Moses and Esther. You win! Amen! You can be assured Athaliah will overpay her hand, until then don't let her see you sweat.

DON'T LET ATHALIAH SEE YOU SWEAT

Paul the apostle offers some especially strategic advice for battle in his epistle to the church at Philippi (Philippians 1:28, AMPC):

And do not [for a moment] be frightened or intimidated in anything by your opponents and adversaries, for such [constancy and fearlessness] will be a clear sign (proof and seal) to them of [their impending] destruction, but [a sure token and evidence] of your deliverance and salvation, and that from God.

In other words, never let Athaliah see you sweat but keep praising God because He has it under control. I like the CEV translation of this verse also:

Be brave when you face your enemies. Your courage will show them that they are going to be destroyed, and it will show you that you will be saved. God will make all of this happen.

Who are your enemies? Not people; not really. The devil, in this case Athaliah, is your enemy. He sometimes uses people to hurt you, but the origin of evil is the devil. If your best friend betrays you, don't show the devil you are disappointed. Pray for those who despitefully use you. If you can't pay your rent, don't stress over your finances. Your God shall supply all of your needs according to His riches in glory by Christ Jesus. If the doctor gives you a bad report, don't speak death over your life. God's name is Jehovah Rapha— the God who heals you. If you just feel like giving up, don't voice your resignation. Jesus will never leave you or forsake you. He'll never give up on you. If you don't quit, you always win.

Don't let Athaliah see you sweat. That doesn't give glory to God. Think about it for a minute. Was Jesus ever for a moment frightened or intimidated in anything by His opponents and adversaries? No, He wasn't. If you are born again, you are in Christ and you have no reason to fear anything or anyone. When a trial comes in your life, the devil is watching and God is watching. Who's going to get the glory? If you get worried and scared, you are giving the devil glory. If you stand in faith, nothing wavering, you are giving God the glory.

When we let Athaliah see us sweat, so to speak, we are demonstrating that we have more fear of the devil than respect of the Lord. When we start talking about all of our problems and walking in worry, we are demonstrating that we have more faith in what the devil is showing us than faith in what the Lord has told us. When we let Athaliah see us sweat, we are not in complete unity with God because we are not walking in His Word.

So how do you keep from caving in under Athaliah's pressure? How do you stand firm in faith when Athaliah's revenge is breaking loose against you? The concept is simple: Look at things from God's perspective and pray. What is God's perspective? God's perspective is in His Word. God doesn't break a sweat when you can't pay a bill. God doesn't start biting his nails when you lose your job. God doesn't have a nervous breakdown when you get a bad report. No, God laughs at Athaliah because He knows the end of your story. You win if you stand in faith!

17

The Sword of David

AFTER YOU GET THE DIVINE STRATEGY to strike Athaliah down, it's time to armor up. Make haste. Run swiftly to the battle line. God has given us the weapons of His warfare, which are not carnal but mighty according to 2 Corinthians 10:4. The master weapon to defeat Athaliah is, not surprisingly, the sword of David.

The sword of David is a sword that represents David's victories and David's way of battle. Remember, David never lost a battle. We have the sword of the spirit, which is the Word of God (see Ephesians 6). But we have to learn how to wield the sword with skill, passion, and humility to defeat Athaliah.

First, you have to understand—or remember—what you are fighting for. If you lose focus of the cause, you will grow weary in battle. Athaliah wants to steal your joy because the joy of the Lord is your strength. If she can steal your joy, she can steal your strength. If she can steal your strength you are more likely to give up. David understood what he was fighting for. He cried, "Is there not a cause?" (1 Samuel 17:29).

BEGIN TO TRAIN FOR BATTLE NOW

Don't wait until you find yourself in a raging war to learn how to fight. Long before David ever fought Goliath—long before he repeatedly routed the Philistine armies—he trained for victory in the wilderness. He developed his warfare skills in the wilderness—and his first victories were against lions and bears attacking his flock.

David confidently told Saul:

Your servant used to keep his father's sheep, and when a lion or a bear came and took a lamb out of the flock, I went out after it and struck it, and delivered the lamb from its mouth; and when it arose against me, I caught it by its beard, and struck and killed it. Your servant has killed both lion and bear; and this uncircumcised Philistine will be like one of them, seeing he has defied the armies of the living God.

1 Samuel 17:34-38

Many people bemoan the wilderness. They are concerned about getting out of the wilderness as fast as possible. David took advantage of his wilderness days and so should you. There will come a day when God promotes you a giant, whether it's Athaliah or some other demonic force, will come against your uprising. Wise ones learn to be worshipping warriors in the wilderness. (You can get spiritual warfare equipping at www.schoolofthespirit.tv.)

DAVID UNDERSTOOD KEY TRUTHS

Sometimes we take spiritual warfare personally, but ultimately this is the Lord's battle we're fighting. We are just His battle-axe. David understood this:

And then all this assembly will know that it is not by sword and spear that the Lord saves. For the battle belongs to the Lord, and He will give you into our hands.

1 Samuel 17:47

132

David understood that, ultimately, the battle he was fighting wasn't his battle. It wasn't even Israel's battle. It was the Lord's battle. This is a key truth that inspires confidence in our hearts. When we see enemies opposing God's will, we can be sure He is fighting for us because we are in covenant with Him.

David understood covenant. Surely, he read about God's covenant with Noah and God's covenant with Abraham and God's covenant with Isaac—and God's covenant with Israel. He understood covenant at a personal level.

Covenant is not well-understood today. The Hebrew word for covenant is *bereeth*. According to The KJV Old Testament Hebrew Lexicon, it means "covenant, alliance, pledge." In the context of a covenant between God and man it means: alliance (of friendship) and "divine ordinance with signs and pledges."

A covenant is "a usually formal, solemn, binding agreement; a written agreement or promise usually under seal between two or more parties especially for the performance of some action" according to *Merriam-Webster*.

In David's days, circumcision was the sign of the covenant. After Goliath cursed David by his gods, his reply demonstrated his faith in a covenant-keeping God:

> *For who is this uncircumcised Philistine that he should defy the armies of the living God?*

> 1 Samuel 17:26

DAVID SOUGHT THE LORD BEFORE BATTLE

David had a habit of asking the Lord for counsel before he ran to a battle line. Although he slaughtered Goliath as a young man, he didn't get prideful in his spiritual warfare skills. He knew if the Lord wasn't fighting for him and through him, he would not win.

"Shall I go up?" Every spiritual warrior needs to ask this question before engaging the enemy. In other words, we need to be led by the Holy Spirit into battle if we want God to lead us into triumph. If we lose a battle, it could very well be that the Holy Spirit didn't lead us into the spiritual skirmish in the first place.

Clearly, there was an injustice underway, but David didn't take it upon himself to bring justice. Rather, he asked his just God this critical question: "'Shall I go and attack these Philistines?' And the Lord said to David, 'Go and attack the Philistines, and save Keilah'" (v. 2).

Although we war from a place of victory, rushing into spiritual warfare outside of God's timing can lead to defeat. Although we are taught to remain on the offensive, presuming to enter a battle God has not called us to fight can be a dangerous mistake.

DAVID SOUGHT CONFIRMATION BEFORE MOVING

When David's men admitted they were afraid to go to battle, he wasn't prideful and presumptuous enough to think he could save the whole city with a sling and a stone just because he did it once before. And he didn't pooh-pooh their fears. Instead, David inquired of the Lord a second time. The Lord gave David the confirmation he was looking for:

Then David again inquired of the Lord. And the Lord answered him and said, "Arise, go down to Keilah because I am giving the Philistines into your hand." Then David and his men went to Keilah. He fought with the Philistines and carried off their livestock, and he struck them with a great slaughter. So David rescued the inhabitants of Keilah.

1 Samuel 23:4-5

There's a good lesson here. Even though God initially told David to go up, he was cautious—and humble enough—to continue seeking the Lord for confirmation when it appeared the circumstances could be changing. He was concerned for the welfare of his men, who were afraid. Instead of rebuking them for flowing in fear, he went back to the Lord to make sure he heard right.

I believe this careful, caring approach is one of the reasons David's men trusted his leadership so much. If you want to be an effective general in God's army, you need to pray about your team's legitimate concerns before heading into battle. That doesn't mean you cower in the face of a challenge. It just means you make doubly—even triply—sure that you are in God's will and that you've counted the costs of waging war before leading others into dangerous territory.

DAVID STAYED HUMBLE IN VICTORY

David built quite a reputation for warfare. In fact, after David defeated Goliath, Saul set the brave teenager over his men of war. When David was coming home from his big win, the women came out of all the cities of Israel. They were singing and dancing and said, "Saul has slain his thousands, and David his ten thousands" (1 Sam. 18:7).

David could have gotten puffed up in the midst of the honor. He could have taken pride in his hand-to-hand combat skills. But he didn't get prideful. The sword of David represents a humble dependence on God that breeds a confidence in your heart that the enemy will fall and His plans will be established for His glory.

18

Dealing with Athaliah's Retaliation

WHEN ATHALIAH IS DEFEATED, the air is clear again. The incessant attacks cease. You can breathe. You can hear the voice of God more clearly. That was Judah's reality under Jehoash. Jehoash restored the throne to David's lineage and he "did what was right in the sight of the Lord all the days in which Jehoiada the priest instructed him" (see 2 Kings 12:2).

Judah prospered under his reign. He repaired the temple, but he too would meet with retaliation. He reigned for 40 years in Judah before the enemy found an opportune time. His own servants rose up against him. 2 Kings 12:20-21 reads:

> *And his servants arose and formed a conspiracy, and killed Joash in the house of the Millo, which goes down to Silla. For Jozachar the son of Shimeath and Jehozabad the son of Shomer, his servants, struck him. So he died, and they buried him with his fathers in the City of David. Then Amaziah his son reigned in his place.*

Chroniclers say Jehoash was murdered in his own bed, revealing that someone had intimate access to him. Before Jehoash was murdered though, he fell into Athaliah's temptation. After the death of his mentor, the priest Jehoiada, he renewed Baal worship in Judah despite prophetic warning after prophetic warning. Jehoash fell into such depravity that he even commanded the murder of the prophet Zechariah. Jehoash opened himself up to the spirits that ruled Athaliah and Jezebel and God allowed the enemy to take him out. What a sad ending to a revivalist king's life.

ATHALIAH ALWAYS RETALIATES

Jesus makes it clear: We are to pray for our enemies and bless those who curse us (see Matthew 5). Paul said bless and curse not (see Romans 12:14). But when Athaliah retaliates against us in spiritual warfare, we don't pray for the demon. We don't bless Athaliah. We deal with the retaliation as soldiers in the army of God.

Although we are supposed to be on the offense, many times demons retaliate against us suddenly and we have to go on the defense to gain the victory before returning to our offensive posture. And there are times when the enemy strikes first, but understand that all enemy attacks are essentially retaliation against God on the inside of you.

What is retaliation? The word *retaliate* means "to repay in kind" or "to return like for like." It's used in the context of taking revenge. Although vengeance belongs to the Lord and He will repay, we have authority in the earth to execute His will against our spiritual enemies. And we are not called to allow the enemy to retaliate against us without a response.

We see a clear tactic of the enemy to retaliate throughout Scripture—and Athaliah is no different. In the Old Testament, Jezebel's children wreaked as much havoc on the kingdom of Israel after her death as the wicked queen did during her reign. Many years after David defeated Goliath, we find four of the giant's descendants intent on taking revenge (2 Samuel 21:18-22).

In the New Testament, we see Luke describe the enemy's strategy. After Jesus was tempted in the wilderness for 40 days, we read: "When the devil had ended all the temptations, he departed from Him until another time" (Luke 4:13). The New International Version describes it as "an opportune time." The New Living Translation says the devil waited until "the next opportunity came." The King James Version says "he departed from him for a season." And Young's Literal Translation says, "he departed from Him till a convenient season."

In this case, the more convenient season was when Jesus was likely in the Garden of Gethsemane. The Bible does not expressly say that Satan was tempting Him, but we know He was battling in His mind because He asked the Lord three times to let the cup of suffering pass from Him and we know he sweat drops of blood from the pressure (see Matthew 26).

Although no weapon formed against God's spiritual warriors can prosper, the enemy nonetheless forms a weapon and takes his best shot. After all, when you take a stand against darkness—when you thwart the enemy's plans—you just did significant damage to the kingdom of darkness.

COMBATTING ATHALIAH'S RETALIATION

We've talked about how and why the enemy retaliates. So what's our response to the retaliation, or what some call spiritual backlash? This thirteen-point action plan will guide you when Athaliah's attack against your mind or body is so great you can't remember what to do. Refer back to it after the battle as you brace for retaliation.

1. Get in the right mindset. When I was younger in the Lord, we saw a lot of retaliation after our annual

November conferences. We saw everything from the inconvenience of flat tires to the devastation of houses catching on fire. We adopted the phrase, "I am the retaliation." Remember that before retaliation ever strikes. You are the retaliation. Greater is He who is in you than he who is in the world (see 1 John 4:4).

2. Expect the retaliation. My first mentor in the prophetic taught me to brace myself for the blow and it won't have as much impact. George Washington once said, "To be prepared for war is one of the most effective means of preserving peace." When you stay on the alert, the enemy can't blindside you.

   Don't think it strange when a trial comes your way after you advance. Peter tells us "think it not strange" (1 Peter 4:12). Other translations say, "Don't be surprised" (NIV) or "don't be astonished" (New Heart English). That Greek word for strange is *xenizo*. According to The KJV New Testament Greek Lexicon" in this context it means, "to surprise or astonish by the strangeness and novelty of a thing; to think strange, be shocked."

   We should not be shocked that the devil retaliates. We should expect it. Don't lay your weapons down. The enemy won't stop advancing against you just because you trade your weapon for a white flag of surrender.

3. Bind the retaliation before it manifests. Again, you have to know that the enemy will retaliate in some way shape or form—unless you remain on the offensive. That's not paranoia. It's common sense. Some of the warfare you find yourself in is retaliation you didn't expect or recognize as such. One way to remain on the offensive

after moving out into the Lord's will is to bind the retaliation.

Remember, Jesus gave us the keys to the kingdom. In Matthew 18:18, Jesus said,

Assuredly, I say to you, whatever you bind on earth will be bound in heaven, and whatever you loose on earth will be loosed in heaven.

I like the AMPC translation of this verse:

Truly I tell you, whatever you forbid and declare to be improper and unlawful on earth must be what is already forbidden in heaven, and whatever you permit and declare proper and lawful on earth must be what is already permitted in heaven.

Here's how you do that: "I bind the hand of Athaliah, in Jesus name. I bind up the retaliation that is forming against me, in the name of the Lord."

Yes, it's just that simple. That's your jumping-off point. The Holy Spirit will lead you to pray further, perhaps binding Athaliah's witchcraft, Athaliah's lies, etc.

4. <u>Walk in the Spirit.</u> We should always, always walk in the spirit but in seasons of spiritual warfare, we need to be overly cautious to walk circumspectly—to walk in the Spirit and not in the flesh. When you find yourself under enemy assault in retaliation, if you are walking in the Spirit you will take the hot air out of his balloon because ultimately, he's after your peace and joy. If you can walk by the principles of the kingdom of God— righteousness, peace and joy in the Holy Spirit—you will more quickly diffuse the enemy's retaliation.

5. <u>Plead the blood of Jesus.</u> As part of going on the offense against demonic retaliation, we plead the blood of Jesus over our minds, bodies, families, finances, and

properties. The blood of Jesus provides spiritual protection.

6. <u>Call in reinforcements.</u> When you are taking ground rapidly for the Lord or when you record a big victory, you need to call in the reinforcements to help you keep the ground you just took. Remember, overcoming Athaliah is a corporate affair—and so is binding and breaking the retaliation.

7. <u>Cut off the enemy's communication devices.</u> Satan is the prince of the power of the air (see Ephesians 2:2). His army is highly organized and demons communicate with one another. You can cut off the enemy's communication devices and send confusion into the enemy's camp to thwart the retaliation.

8. <u>Cancel enemy assignments.</u> Take the time right after a victory to cancel every enemy assignment and dismantle every enemy weapon of retaliation being formed against you, in Jesus' name. Many warriors forget this, just like some gym rats forget to stretch after a hard workout. The next day, their muscles retaliated and they were sorry they didn't stretch.

9. <u>Blind watching and listening spirits.</u> Just like there are watcher angels and angels who record our words, there are watcher demons and demonic entities that listen for our words—looking to find agreement with vain imaginations the enemy whispers into our mind. I teach about monitoring spirits intensively at School of the Seers at www.schoolofthespirit.tv. You want to take authority over monitoring spirits spying on you.

10. <u>Release God's angels.</u> Release God's angels to war, protect and preserve. Psalm 103:20 says, "Bless the

Lord, you His angels, who are mighty, and do His commands, and obey the voice of His word." The Passion Translation of this verse says, "So bless the Lord, all his messengers of power, for you are his mighty heroes who listen intently to the voice of his word to do it."

11. <u>Don't get upset that you are under attack.</u> Don't feel like a victim in the face of backlash. Don't whine and complain about what the enemy is doing. Don't have a pity party. Pity parties attract demons. You are not a victim. You are victorious in Christ. Watch your words. Let your tongue cleave to the roof of your mouth if you can't praise him. Bite your tongue no matter how much pressure the enemy puts on you to speak words of death over your life.

12. <u>Don't show Athaliah any weakness whatsoever.</u> While there are times when you just need to retreat and recoup and rest if you are severely ill, as much as you can help it don't back down in the area of attack or the enemy will just keep hitting you in those weak spots. In other words, if you let a headache keep you out of church you'll get headaches every Sunday morning.

These words of apostolic advice in Philippians 1:27-28 drive home the point: "Only let your conduct be worthy of the gospel of Christ, so that whether I come and see you or am absent, I may hear of your affairs, that you stand fast in one spirit, with one mind striving together for the faith of the gospel, and not in any way terrified by your adversaries, which is to them a proof of perdition, but to you of salvation, and that from God."

13. <u>Don't fear Athaliah's retaliation.</u> When you do battle, don't fear Athaliah's retaliation. Fear opens the door to demonic attack. Athaliah wants you to fear her retaliation so that you won't take a stand. Don't fool yourself. If you don't take a stand, she won't back down.

Often Athaliah will whisper threats to your heart to intimidate you from running to the battle line. Don't fall for it. Instead of fearing the retaliation, become the retaliation. God didn't give you a spirit of fear, but of power, love, and a sound mind (see 2 Timothy 1:7). Instead of walking in a defensive posture, go on the offense and stay there.

Epilogue

A Prayer to
Strike Down Athaliah

I HAVE OVERCOME ATHALIAH time and time again—and you can, too. You've got the prophetic intelligence you need to succeed in this battle. You've got principles of strategies that have worked in the past. And you have the Holy Spirit who will show you the particulars of the specific battle you are in. Before you charge out to battle, though, I wanted to give you a model prayer. Don't take this rotely, but do read it out loud when you've lost words. Let's face it. Sometimes the witchcraft attacks are so strong you need some help. I trust this prayer will help you.

> Father, in the name of Jesus, I repent for tolerating Athaliah, Ahab, Jezebel, or any other spirits that have come to steal, kill and destroy in my life, my loved ones, my finances, my health, or any other aspect of the life you died to give me. I reject and renounce all agreement with Athaliah. I ask you to forgive me for tolerating or maintaining agreement in my heart with darkness in all its manifestations. Forgive me for being ignorant of Athaliah's devices. Cleanse me, Lord, from this unrighteousness and wash me white as snow.

> Thank You for the information, revelation, and understanding you have given me about this spirit we call Athaliah. Thank You for showing me in your

Word the danger of this devil and the strategies to guard against it and to strike it down when it rises up against me. Father, help me to get these truths deep in my spirit so when the attack comes I am a doer of the Word that I've heard. Let this truth come alive in me so that I am sharp and sensitive to any coming danger in the spirit.

Lord, help me connect the dots that Athaliah is drawing in the spirit. Help me see her maneuvers in the spirit before they manifest in the natural. Increase my discernment in the spirit realm and help me identify disturbances to the peace you've given me. Teach me even more about how to overcome this spirit and help me not to go into battle without asking you for the specific plan for the war I face. Lord, give me more and more revelation into the ways of Athaliah so I can escape the surprise attacks—the ambushes that blindside me.

Lord, be my shield and buckler in every battle with Athaliah. I plead the blood of Jesus over myself and everything that you have given me to steward. I decree Athaliah will not steal my inheritance. I plead the blood of Jesus against Athaliah. I draw a bloodline in the spirit. I decree I will not be blindsided because I am sensitive to the Holy Spirit and He will show me things to come—and the weapons that Athaliah is forming against me. I decree I will strike down Athaliah with the sword of David every time she comes my way. I shall wield the sword with great humility in total dependence on your authority and power, in Jesus' name. I am the retaliation.

I command Athaliah's witchcraft to be broken over my life. I spoil the weapons of Athaliah with the Word of God. I command Athaliah's evil devices to bow, in the name of Jesus, and I decree Athaliah's threats and curses are deactivated in my life. I decree Athaliah's tongues are condemned. I decree the blessings of God chase me down and overtake me. I say I am blessed coming in and blessed going out.

I release double fire against demonic tag teams plotting against me. I sever their cords and break their bands in Jesus' name. I decree that I reign in life with Christ Jesus. I am the head and not the tail, above and not beneath. I walk in breakthrough because the Breaker, Jesus, lives on the inside of me. The power that raised Christ from the dead dwells on the inside of me. I am strong in the Lord and the power of His might, in Jesus' name. Amen.

CPSIA information can be obtained
at www.ICGtesting.com
Printed in the USA
LVHW050801150321
681563LV00023B/1322